GW01007647

New Present Day English   Book 1

New Present Day English

E. Frank Candlin

Formerly Principal of the Oxford College of Further Education

Book 1

HODDER AND STOUGHTON
LONDON SYDNEY AUCKLAND TORONTO

ISBN 0 340 15668 6

Copyright © 1972 E. Frank Candlin
Eighteenth impression 1985
Illustrations copyright © 1972 Hodder and Stoughton Ltd

All rights reserved. No part of this publication may be
reproduced or transmitted in any form or by any means,
electronic or mechanical, including photocopy, recording,
or any information storage and retrieval system, without .
permission in writing from the publisher

Illustrations by Bill Burnard

Printed in Great Britain for
Hodder and Stoughton Educational,
a division of Hodder and Stoughton Ltd,
Mill Road, Dunton Green, Sevenoaks, Kent,
by Hazell Watson & Viney Limited,
Member of the BPCC Group,
Aylesbury, Bucks

Contents

Preface

This edition of *New Present Day English* has been rewritten to take account of recent advances in the theory and practice of teaching English as a foreign language.

The number of lesson units and the number of separate teaching items have both been reduced so that the material of Book One may be covered in the usual academic year of about thirty-six weeks. Narrative and conversation passages have been retained, but they have been made more realistic, with an increased emphasis on the interests of young people. Numerous examples of the new structures to be presented in each unit have been included in the dialogues and reading passages and the exercises have been made more varied, stimulating and contextual. These may be supplemented by the *New Present Day English Work Books*.

Much more use has been made of illustrations, which are designed to stimulate vocabulary-building and oral work in the classroom as well as to enliven the text.

The controlled vocabulary—some 750 words in Book One, only about 50 of which are not in the General Service Word List—is given at the end. There is an easy reference index to the exercises and a list of the sentence patterns giving the teaching point covered and an example of each. Throughout the book nothing is taken for granted except what has been covered in earlier units. Phonetic transcripts are given for all new words as they occur, and again in the general vocabulary. The standard I. P. A. symbols replace the simplified forms used in earlier editions. In the second half of the book a short anecdote in lighter vein has been added at the end of each unit.

Advice on the best method of using *New Present Day English* together with detailed teaching notes for each unit will be found in *Teacher's Book One*. Teaching English as a foreign or second language is a highly skilled art, particularly when rapid results are looked for. It is hoped that this course, based on long practical experience, will make the task easier for the teacher and more enjoyable for the student.

E. F. C.

Key to Phonetic Symbols

Vowels and Diphthongs

iː	siː	see	ðiːz	these
i	siks	six	θin	thin
e	ten	ten	sed	said
æ	hæd	had	pæk	pack
ɑː	hɑːd	hard	fɑːst	fast
ɔ	hɔt	hot	wɔt	what
ɔː	dɔː	door	kɔːt	caught
u	tuk	took	put	put
uː	buːt	boot	juː	you
ʌ	sʌn	son	kʌt	cut
əː	səː	sir	fəːst	first
ə	'mʌðə	mother	'sistə	sister
ei	keim	came	eit	eight
ou	ʃou	show	nou	no
ai	lait	light	nain	nine
au	kau	cow	raund	round
ɔi	tɔi	toy	bɔi	boy
iə	niə	near	hiə	here
ɛə	pɛə	pair	wɛə	where
uə	ʃuə	sure	juə	you're

Consonants

t	teik	take	put	put
d	dɔg	dog	hæd	had
p	pen	pen	mæp	map
b	buk	book	'teibl	table
k	'kɔfi	coffee	buk	book
g	gou	go	dɔg	dog
f	fɔː	four	hɑːf	half
v	'veri	very	hæv	have
m	'mʌðə	mother	kʌm	come
n	nain	nine	hænd	hand
ŋ	siŋ	sing	'rʌniŋ	running
l	luk	look	dɔl	doll
θ	θin	thin	sauθ	south
ð	ðis	this	'fɑːðə	father
s	siks	six	buks	books

z	rouz	rose	dɔgz	dogs
ʃ	ʃæl	shall	fiʃ	fish
ʒ	'pleʒə	pleasure	'viʒn	vision
tʃ	mætʃ	match	'kwestʃn	question
dʒ	bridʒ	bridge	peidʒ	page
r	rʌn	run	tə'mɔrou	tomorrow
w	wɔːl	wall	wen	when
j	jiə	year	jes	yes
h	hænd	hand	hɔt	hot

Unit 1

John and Mary Brown

JOHN: Hello, Mary.
MARY: Hello, John. What's this?
JOHN: It's a book. What's that? Is it a pen?
MARY: No, it isn't. It's a pencil.

MARY: What's that, John?
JOHN: It's a bird.

This is a man.
This is John Brown.
John Brown's a man.
He's a man.

This is a woman.
This is Mary Brown.
Mary Brown's a woman.
She's a woman.

MARY: What's that, John?
JOHN: What's that?
MARY: Yes, John. What's that? Is it a man?
JOHN: No, it isn't. It's a dog.

New Words

a bird (bəːd)
a book (buk)
a chair (tʃɛə)
a cigarette (sigəˈret)
a dog (dɔg)
a door (dɔː)
a man (mæn)
a pen (pen)
a pencil ('pensil)
a picture ('piktʃə)
a table ('teibl)
a wall (wɔːl)
a window ('windou)
a woman ('wumən)

John Brown ('dzɔn 'braun)
Mary Brown ('mɛəri 'braun)

am (æm, əm, m)
are (ɑː)
is (iz)

he (hiː, hi)
I (ai)
it (it)
she (ʃiː, ʃi)
they (ðei)
you (juː, ju)

this (ðis)

that (ðæt)
these (ðiːz)
those (ðouz)

a (ə)
and (ænd, ənd, ən)

hello! (heˈlou)
no (nou)
not (nɔt)
what? (wɔt)
yes (jes)

Sentence Patterns

1

This is / That's / It's	a door. / a wall. / a table. / a window.

These are / Those are / They're	doors. / walls. / windows. / tables.

2

What's this? / What's that?	

It's	a cigarette. / a dog. / a window.

What are these / What are those?	

They're	cigarettes. / dogs. / windows.

3

Is this / Is that / Is it	a man? / a woman? / a dog? / a wall? / a door?

Yes, it is. / No, it isn't.

Are these / Are those / Are they	dogs? / doors? / chairs? / tables? / pens?

Yes, they are. / No, they aren't.

4 He's a man.
  I'm a man.

She's a woman.
You're a woman.

Exercises

A. 1 What's this?

2 What's this?

3 What's this?

4 What's this?

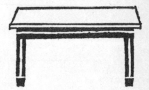

5 What are these?

6 What are these?

7 What are these?

8 What are these?

B. *Yes, it is.   No, it isn't.   Yes, they are.   No, they aren't.*

1   Is this a chair?
    Is it a table?

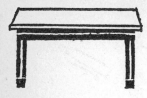

2   Is this a table?
    Is it a book?

3   Is this a pencil?
    Is it a pen?

4   Is this a man?
    Is it a woman?

5   Are these walls?
    Are they windows?

6   Are these books?
    Are they pictures?

7   Are these pencils?
    Are they pens?

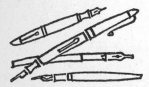

8   Are these dogs?
    Are they birds?

C. *Write this:*

This is John Brown.   This is Mary Brown.
What's that?   It's a picture.
What are those?   They're pencils.
Is this a bird?   Yes, it is.

Unit 2

In the Sitting-room

This is a table.

This is a bag.

The bag is on the table; it's on the table.

This is a dog.

The dog is under the table.

Where's the dog? It's under the table.

It isn't *on* the table; it's *under* the table.

 This is a picture.

This is a wall.

The picture is on the wall.
Where's the picture?
It's on the wall.

 This is a chair.

The chair is under the picture.

The picture is on the wall, and the chair is under the picture.

This is a man.
His name is John Brown; he's Mr Brown.
He has got a book in his hand.
He hasn't got a pen in his hand.
He's got a cigarette in his mouth.

This is a woman.
Her name is Mary Brown; she's Mrs Brown.
She has got a pen in her hand.
She hasn't got a cigarette in her mouth.

This is a sitting-room. John and Mary Brown are in the sitting-room; it's their sitting-room. The sitting-room is in their house.

JOHN: Where's my pen, Mary?

MARY: I've got a pen in my bag; it's my pen.

JOHN: Where's your bag?

MARY: It's on the table.

JOHN: You haven't got a pen in your bag. This isn't a pen; it's a pencil. Where's my pen?

MARY: Oh, John. Your pen's on the table, under my bag.

JOHN: Where's our dog? Where's Toby?

MARY: He's under the table. Where's my book?

JOHN: Is this your book?

MARY: No, it isn't. My book's on this chair.

Look at the picture above. Answer these questions:

1 Where are Mr and Mrs Brown?

2 Where is their sitting-room?

3 What has Mr Brown got in his hand?

4 Is their dog in the room?

5 Where is the dog?

6 Is Mr Brown in his chair?

7 Where are the pictures?

8 Has Mr Brown got a cigarette in his mouth?

9 Has Mrs Brown got a book in her hand?

New Words

a bag (bæg)	his (hiz)
a hand (hænd)	her (həː, hə)
a house (haus)	my (mai)
a mouth (mauθ)	our (auə)
a name (neim)	their (ðɛə)
a room (ruːm)	your (jɔː, jə)
a sitting-room ('sitiŋruːm)	we (wiː, wi)
Mr ('mistə)	
Mrs ('misiz)	in (in)
Toby ('toubi)	on (ɔn)
	under ('ʌndə)
got (gɔt)	
has (hæz)	the (ðə, ði)
have (hæv)	where? (wɛə)

Sentence Patterns

5 This is a man. The man is Mr Brown.
This is a woman. The woman is Mrs Brown.
This is a room; this is a house. The room is in the house.
This is a picture; this is a wall. The picture is on the wall.
This is a bag; this is a table. The bag is on the table.

6

	am	I?
Where	is	Mr Brown? he? Mrs Brown? she? the book? it?
	are	we? you? they? Mr and Mrs Brown? the books?

7

I	am / 'm	in the room. in the house.
He She	is / 's	
The book It		on the table. under the table.
We You They	are / 're	in the room. in the house.
The books They		on the table. under the table.

8 (a)

I You We Mr and Mrs Brown They	have have not haven't	got	a book. a pen. a cigarette.
John He Mary She	has has not hasn't		
The room It			a window. a door.

(b)

Have	you Mr and Mrs Brown they	got	a room? a house? a dog?
Has	John he Mary she		
	the room it		a window? a door?

(c)

Yes,	I we they	have.
	he she it	has.

No,	I we they	haven't.
	he she it	hasn't.

9

I					
You	have 've			my your	
We		got	a table a chair a picture	our	house.
They				their	
He	has 's			his	
She				her	

10

Question	Answer
What have I got in my hand?	You've got a pen in your hand. A pen.
What have you got in your hand?	I've got a book in my hand. A book.
What has he got in his hand?	He's got a bag in his hand. A bag.
What has she got in her hand?	She's got a pencil in her hand. A pencil.
What have they got in their sitting-room?	They've got a picture in their sitting-room. A picture.

Exercises

A. 1 Mr and Mrs Brown (*has, have*) got a house; they've got a sitting-room (*on, under, in*) (*his, her, their*) house.

2 Mr and Mrs Brown are (*in, on, under*) (*his, their, her*) sitting-room.

3 Mrs Brown has got a pen (*under, on, in*) her hand.

4 (*Her, his, their*) bag is
(*under, in, on*) the table.

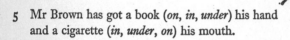

5 Mr Brown has got a book (*on, in, under*) his hand
and a cigarette (*in, under, on*) his mouth.

6 Their dog is (*under, in, on*) the table.

7 (*Their, his, her*) name is Toby.

B. *Finish this:*

I			a book	in		hand.
	have		a sitting-room		our	house.
Mrs Brown			a picture			wall.
Mr Brown			a cigarette	in	his	
They		got	a dog	in	their	sitting-room.
			a bag	in	her	
	have		a pen	in	your	bag.

C. *Write this:*

*I am ----- (your name). This is my book. My book is
on the table. I have got a pen in my hand. This
is my pen. Have you got a pen in your bag?*

29

Unit 3

The Browns at Breakfast

Mr and Mrs Brown are in their dining-room. The dining-room is in their house. They've got a son and a daughter.

David is their son; he's a boy.

Susan is their daughter; she's a girl.

David is tall; he's a tall boy. Susan is his sister. Susan isn't tall; she isn't a tall girl. She's pretty; she's a pretty girl. David is her brother.

Now David and Susan are sitting on chairs near the table. They are eating their breakfast. They are eating bacon and eggs.

David has got a cup and saucer a plate a knife

a fork and a spoon.

They've got bread and butter and marmalade on the table. They've got cups and saucers, plates, knives, forks and spoons on the table too. The Browns are having their breakfast. Mr and Mrs Brown are the father and mother; David and Susan are their son and daughter. Toby is their dog.

Mr Brown isn't sitting down; he's standing up near the fire. He's not eating his breakfast now; he isn't hungry.

Mrs Brown isn't eating her breakfast; she's reading a letter. The letter is in her hand.

Their dog is on the carpet near the table; its name is Toby. The dog isn't big; it's not a big dog. It's little; it's a little dog.

Susan is speaking to David. David isn't speaking to Susan. He's eating his breakfast; he's hungry.
Now Mr Brown is walking to the table. He's sitting down on a chair. He's eating his breakfast; he's hungry now.

MR BROWN: What's that, Mary?

MRS BROWN: It's a letter. I'm reading a letter. Sit down, John, and have your breakfast. Aren't you hungry?

MR BROWN: No, I'm not. Where's the dog? Where's Toby?

MRS BROWN: He's there. He's on the carpet, near Susan.

SUSAN: I haven't got a spoon, Mother.

MRS BROWN: Yes, you have. Your spoon's there. It's on the table near your plate. You've got a big spoon and a little spoon.

SUSAN: Oh, yes, they're here. Are you hungry, David?

DAVID: Yes, I am. I'm eating a big breakfast. Is this your cup, Susan?

SUSAN: No, it isn't; it's your cup. This is my cup here, near my plate.

DAVID: You aren't eating your breakfast, Father. Aren't you hungry?

MR BROWN: No, I'm not. You're having a big breakfast, David. What are you eating?

DAVID: I'm eating bacon and eggs, and I'm drinking coffee.

MR BROWN: Are you eating bacon and eggs, Susan?

SUSAN: No, I'm not. I'm eating bread and butter and marmalade.

DAVID: Marmalade! Where's the marmalade? Pass the marmalade, please.

SUSAN: It's here on the table, near my cup and saucer.

MRS BROWN: Are you eating your breakfast, Susan?

SUSAN: Yes, Mother. You aren't eating; what are you doing?

MRS BROWN: I'm reading a letter.

DAVID: I'm not reading a letter; I'm eating my breakfast—a big breakfast. Where's my knife, please, Susan?

SUSAN: It's there, David—on the table, near your plate. You've got a big knife and a little knife.

DAVID: Oh, yes, they're here. Pass the butter, please.

MRS BROWN: Are you hungry now, John?

MR BROWN: Yes, I am.

MRS BROWN: Sit down and eat your breakfast. It's on the table.

MR BROWN: Pass the coffee, please.

MRS BROWN: You've got coffee in your cup.

MR BROWN: Oh, yes. *You're* having a good breakfast, David.

DAVID: Yes, Father, I am.

Answer these questions:

1 Where are the Browns eating their breakfast?
2 Where is Mr Brown standing?
3 What is Mrs Brown reading?
4 What is David doing?
5 Where is their dog?
6 What is Susan eating?
7 Is David reading a letter?
8 Has Mrs Brown got a letter in her hand?
9 What has Mr Brown got in his cup?

New Words

bacon ('beikən)
a boy (bɔi)
bread (bred)
breakfast ('brekfəst)
a brother ('brʌðə)
butter ('bʌtə)
a carpet ('kɑːpit)
coffee ('kɔfi)
a cup (kʌp)
a daughter ('dɔːtə)
a dining-room ('daininɡruːm)
an egg (eg)
a father ('fɑːðə)
a fire (faiə)
a fork (fɔːk)
a girl (gəːl)
a knife, knives (naif, naivz)

a letter ('letə)
marmalade ('mɑːməleid)
a mother ('mʌðə)
a plate (pleit)
a saucer ('sɔːsə)
a sister ('sistə)
a son (sʌn)
a spoon (spuːn)
David ('deivid)
Susan ('suːzn)

to do (duː)
doing ('duːiŋ)
to drink (driŋk)
drinking ('driŋkiŋ)
to eat (iːt)
eating ('iːtiŋ)

to have (hæv)
   having ('hævɪŋ)
to pass (pɑːs)
   passing ('pɑːsɪŋ)
to read (riːd)
   reading ('riːdɪŋ)
to sit (sit)
   sitting ('sitɪŋ)
to speak (spiːk)
   speaking ('spiːkɪŋ)
to stand (stænd)
   standing ('stændɪŋ)
to walk (wɔːk)
   walking ('wɔːkɪŋ)

   its (its)

big (big)
good (gud)
hungry ('hʌŋgri)
little ('litl)
pretty ('priti)
tall (tɔːl)

an (ən)
down (daun)
here (hiə)
near (niə)
now (nau)
please (pliːz)
there (ðɛə)
to (tu, tə)
too (tuː)
up (ʌp)

Sentence Patterns

11 Adjectives

David is tall.	He's a tall boy.
Susan is pretty.	She's a pretty girl.
Mr Brown is hungry.	He's a hungry man.
Their dog is little.	It's a little dog.
The house is big.	It's a big house.

12 Present Continuous tense *(a)*

I	am 'm am not 'm not	
David and Susan They You We	are aren't	sitting near the table. reading a letter. standing near the fire. drinking coffee.
David He Susan She	is isn't	
The dog It		sitting on the carpet.

(b)

Am	I	
Are	David and Susan they you we	sitting near the table? reading a letter? standing near the fire? drinking coffee?
Is	David he Susan she	
	the dog it	sitting on the carpet?

(c)

Yes,	I	am.
	you they we	are.
	he she it	is.

No,	I	am not. 'm not.
	you they we	are not. aren't.
	he she it	is not. isn't.

13 Imperative

Sit down.
Pass the marmalade, please.
Pass the butter, please.
Drink your coffee, Susan.
Eat your breakfast.

Exercises

A. *Finish these sentences:*

1 The Browns are ...
2 Mr Brown is ... near the ...
3 Mrs Brown is ... a ...
4 Susan is ... to David.
5 The dog is on the ... near the ...
6 Mrs Brown isn't ...
7 Mr and Mrs Brown have got a ... and a ...
8 Susan is drinking ...
9 David is eating ... and ...
10 Is David ... his ...?

B. *Make questions:*

1 The Browns are in their sitting-room.
2 They are eating their breakfast.
3 Susan and David are sitting near the table.
4 David is hungry.
5 Mrs Brown is reading a letter.
6 Their dog is under the table.

C. *Make sentences with these words:*

1 Susan, girl, pretty

2 Mr Brown, man, tall

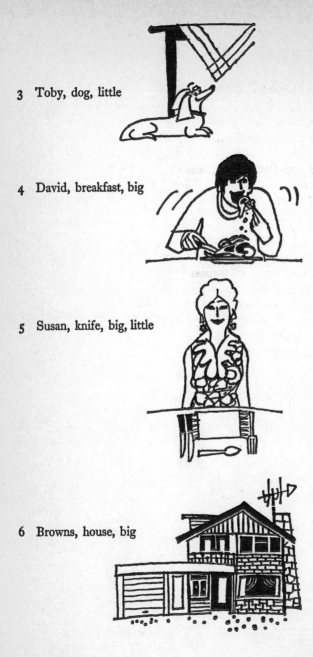

3 Toby, dog, little

4 David, breakfast, big

5 Susan, knife, big, little

6 Browns, house, big

7 David, boy, hungry

Unit 4

Saying Good-bye

This is Mr Brown's car.
The car is new; it's a new car.
It's an English car—a Rover.

Mr Brown is sitting in his car.
David is putting a bag into the
car; it's Mr Brown's bag.

Mrs Brown is standing near the
gate.
She's waving her hand and
saying good-bye to her husband.

The postman is giving a letter
to Susan; it's Susan's letter.
She's taking the letter from the
postman and saying, 'Thank
you.'

Who is David?
He's Susan's brother.
Who is Susan?
She's David's sister.

Who is John Brown?
He's Mary Brown's husband.
Who is Mary Brown?
She's John Brown's wife.

Who are David and Susan? They're Mr and Mrs Brown's son and daughter.

MR BROWN: I'm going now, Mary.

MRS BROWN: Have you got your hat and coat, John?

MR BROWN: Yes, thank you. I haven't got my bag: where is it, please?

MRS BROWN: David's got it.

MR BROWN: Where's David? Put my bag into the car, please, David.

DAVID: Yes, Father, I'm putting it into the car.

MR BROWN: Susan's taking a letter from the postman. Is it my letter?

SUSAN: No, Father, it's my letter. It's from Tom Smith.

MRS BROWN: Are you warm or cold, John? Put your coat on.

MR BROWN: I'm warm, thank you. I've got my coat and hat and gloves. And the car's warm, too.

MRS BROWN: Are they your old gloves?
MR BROWN: Yes, they are.
MRS BROWN: Take them off. Put your new gloves on.
They're here.
SUSAN: Where's the dog? Where's Toby?
DAVID: He's in the house.
MR BROWN: Good-bye, Mary. Good-bye, David.
Good-bye, Susan.
MRS BROWN: Good-bye, John.
SUSAN: } Good-bye, Father.
DAVID: }
SUSAN: Has Father got his bag, Mother?
MRS BROWN: Yes, it's in the car.

Answer these questions:

1 What is Mr Brown doing?
2 What is Mrs Brown doing?
3 What is David doing?
4 What has Susan got in her hand?
5 Where is their dog?
6 Who is giving a letter to Susan?
7 Is Mr Brown's car old or new?
8 Is Mr Brown warm or cold?
9 Who is Mr Brown's son?
10 Who is Susan's mother?

New Words

a car (kɑː)
a coat (kout)
a gate (geit)
a glove (glʌv)
a hat (hæt)
a husband ('hʌzbənd)
a postman ('poustmən)
a wife (waif)
a Rover ('rouvə)
Tom Smith ('tom 'smiθ)

to give (giv)
  giving ('giviŋ)
to go (gou)
  going ('gouiŋ)
to put (put)
  putting ('putiŋ)
to say (sei)
  saying ('seiiŋ)
to take (teik)
  taking ('teikiŋ)
to wave (weiv)
  waving ('weiviŋ)

who? (huː)

cold (kould)
English ('iŋgliʃ)
new (njuː)
old (ould)
warm (wɔːm)

from (frɔm, frəm)
into ('intu)
or (ɔː)
good-bye (gud'bai)
thank you ('θæŋkjuː)
them (ðem)

Sentence Patterns

14 Possessive of Nouns

This is Mr Brown's car.
That's Mr Brown's hat.
These are Susan's gloves.
Where's Tom's letter?
Where are John Brown's gloves?
Susan's gloves are on the table.
David's bag is in the car.
Who is Mrs Brown's daughter?
Mr Brown is David's father.
Is this Mr and Mrs Brown's house?
David and Susan are Mr and Mrs Brown's son and daughter.

15 Who?

Who is Mr Brown? (He's) Mrs Brown's husband.
Who is Mrs Brown? (She's) Mr Brown's wife.

Who is David's father? Mr Brown (is David's father).
Who is Susan's mother? Mrs Brown (is Susan's mother).

Who is sitting in the car? Mr Brown (is sitting in the car).
Who is waving good-bye? Mrs Brown (is waving good-bye).

16

The postman is giving a letter to Susan.
Susan is taking a letter from the postman.
David is putting a bag into the car.
Mrs Brown is putting a book on the table.
The dog is eating its breakfast under the table.
David is putting a spoon near his plate.

Unit 4

Exercises

A. Put these words into the sentences:

tall, hungry, pretty, old, new, warm, cold, big, little

    Example: Susan ... girl.
    Susan is a pretty girl.

1 Mr Brown ... car.
2 Toby ... dog.
3 Mr Brown ... gloves.
4 The Browns ... house.
5 Mrs Brown ... coat.
6 David ... boy.
7 Mr Brown ... man.
8 My coffee ...

B. Answer these questions:

1 What is your name?
2 Are you a man or a woman, a boy or a girl?
3 Are you sitting or standing now?
4 What have you got in your hand?
5 Are you warm or cold now?
6 Have you got a car?
7 Have you got a brother or a sister?
8 Who is sitting or standing near you?

Unit 5

Going to the Town

This is Tom Smith. He is Susan's boy-friend.

Tom has a fast car. It's a Jaguar.

Yesterday Tom was in London, but today he is with Susan in his car. They are going to the town, to the shops. Susan is talking to Tom; she is very happy.

Yesterday she wasn't happy. She was at home and in bed. She was cold; she wasn't well.

Now they are driving down the street to the town. They are going to the shops. A policeman is standing in the street; he is putting up his hand and stopping the cars. Boys and girls are walking across the street. Near the pillar-box in this picture is the postman. Yesterday he was in front of Mr Brown's house. He had a letter for Susan. Now he is taking letters from the pillar-box. He is saying, 'Good morning,' to Susan and Tom.

Tom is stopping his car. He is talking to a friend; his friend's name is Jim Blake. Tom is tall and thin, but Jim Blake is short and fat. Jim has a newspaper in his hand.

Tom and Susan and Jim Blake are drinking coffee and eating little cakes in a shop. They were cold in the street but now they are warm.

SUSAN: Where are we going, Tom?

TOM: Into the town—to the shops.

SUSAN: This is a very fast car. Please be careful! Don't drive so fast.

TOM: All right. Now here's a policeman; he's stopping the cars.

SUSAN: Stop, Tom. That's Jim Blake. He's standing there, near the policeman. He's got a newspaper in his hand.

TOM: Yes, it is Jim. Hello, Jim! Where are you going?

JIM: To the town. I'm walking.

TOM: Don't walk into town. Come in our car.

JIM: Thank you. Is this a new car?

TOM: Yes. And it's a very fast car, too. I had an old car; it was very slow. Now I've got a new car, and it's fast.

JIM: This is a Jaguar. They're very good cars. Were you in the town yesterday?

SUSAN: No, we weren't. I wasn't very well. I was in bed.

JIM: I'm sorry. Are you all right now?

SUSAN: Yes, thank you. Stop here, Tom. Here's a good shop; they're selling coffee and cakes. Hurry up! I'm hungry.

TOM: All right! Here's a table near the window. Sit down.

Answer these questions:

1 Where are Tom and Susan going?
2 What is the policeman doing?
3 Where was Susan yesterday?
4 Who is Jim Blake?
5 What has Jim Blake got in his hand?
6 What is the postman doing?
7 What are the boys and girls doing?
8 What car is Tom driving?
9 Where was Tom yesterday?
10 What are they eating in the shop?

New Words

a bed (bed)

a boy-friend ('bɔifrend)

a cake (keik)

a friend (frend)

a home (houm)

a morning ('mɔːniŋ)

a newspaper ('njuːzpeipə)

a pillar-box ('piləbɔks)

a policeman (pə'liːsmən)

a shop (ʃɔp)

a street (striːt)

a town (taun)

a Jaguar ('dʒægjuə)

  Jim Blake ('dʒim 'bleik)

  London ('lʌndən)

to come (kʌm)

  coming ('kʌmiŋ)

to drive (draiv)

  driving ('draiviŋ)

to hurry ('hʌri)

  hurrying ('hʌriiŋ)

  had (hæd)

to sell (sel)

  selling ('seliŋ)

to stop (stɔp)

  stopping ('stɔpiŋ)

to talk (tɔːk)

  talking ('tɔːkiŋ)

  was (wɔz, wəz)

  were (wəː, wə)

careful ('kɛəfl)

fast (fɑːst)

fat (fæt)

happy ('hæpi)

right (rait)

short (ʃɔːt)

slow (slou)

sorry ('sɔri)

thin (θin)

very ('veri)

well (wel)

across (ə'krɔs)

for (fɔː, fə)

in front of (in 'frʌnt əv)

with (wið)

all (ɔːl)

but (bʌt, bət)

so (sou)

today (tə'dei)

yesterday ('jestədi)

all right ('ɔːl 'rait)

at home (ət 'houm)

Be careful! (bi 'kɛəful)

Hurry up! ('hʌri 'ʌp)

Good morning! (gud 'mɔːniŋ)

in bed (in'bed)

Sentence Patterns

17 (*a*)

Mr Brown He Mrs Brown She I	was wasn't	in Tom's car in our house	yesterday.
Tom and David We You They These books	were weren't		

(*b*)

Was David in Mr Brown's car?	Yes, he was.	No, he wasn't.
Was Susan at home yesterday?	Yes, she was.	No, she wasn't.
Was my bag in your car?	Yes, it was.	No, it wasn't.
Were the Browns in London yesterday?	Yes, they were.	No, they weren't.
Were you in Tom's house yesterday?	Yes, I was.	No, I wasn't.
Were my cigarettes on that table yesterday?	Yes, they were.	No, they weren't.

18 Imperative—Negative

Don't drive so fast.
Don't walk into the town.
Don't stop your car here.
Don't put my bag into the car.
Don't stand so near the fire.

Exercises

A. *Make negative sentences with these words:*

Example: Susan, driving, car
Susan isn't driving Tom's car.

1 Susan, well, yesterday
2 Tom, London, today
3 the Browns, home, yesterday
4 policeman, stopping, cars, street

5 Jim Blake, house, London
6 Mr Brown, bag, car, yesterday
7 David, hungry, today
8 he, eating, breakfast
9 these, my, books

B. *Put in the right words:*

Tom Smith is driving ... the town ... his car ... Susan. A policeman is standing ... the pillar-box; he is putting ... his hand, and cars are stopping ... the policeman. Boys and girls are walking ... the street. The postman is taking letters ... the pillar-box. Has he got a letter ... Susan? Yes, he has got a letter ... Tom. Susan is ... Tom's car now.

Unit 6

At the Railway Station

This is a railway station. In this picture there are nine people. There is a man coming through the gate from the platform. A man at the gate is taking tickets. A porter is carrying three large bags to the train. There is a woman with the porter; she is carrying one small bag in her hand. She is hurrying to the train. She has a black coat and hat and white gloves, and she is carrying an umbrella. A man and a woman are on the platform near the train; they are talking and waving good-bye to their friends on the train. A porter is closing the doors.

Mr Brown and his friend came to the station by car. Mr Brown saw his friend, Mr Fred Brook, in the street and brought him to the station. He drove his car to the station and left it outside.

Mr Brown went to the booking-office and got his ticket, and Mr Brook bought cigarettes and a box of matches. Yesterday their train was late, but today it is standing in the station.

Mr Brown and his friend ran through the gate to platform five. The porter opened the door; they got into the train and sat down. Now the porter is closing the door and the train is leaving the station.

MR BROWN:	One ticket to London, please.
BOOKING-CLERK:	Single or return?
MR BROWN:	Return, please.
BOOKING-CLERK:	Are you going today, sir?
MR BROWN:	Yes.
BOOKING-CLERK:	There's a train to London in the station now. Platform five.

MR BROOK:	A packet of cigarettes, please.
GIRL (*selling cigarettes*):	How many? Ten, sir?
MR BROOK:	Yes, please. And a box of matches.
GIRL:	Here they are. Thank you.
MR BROOK:	Thank you. Good morning.

PORTER: Are you going to London, madam?

WOMAN: Yes, I am.

PORTER: Your train's standing in the station. Is this your luggage? Three bags?

WOMAN: Yes. There are two large bags and one small bag. I'm going to my friend's house in London.

PORTER: Have you got your ticket?

WOMAN: Yes, it's in my bag.

PORTER: Good. The train's there on platform five. Through that gate, madam.

MR BROWN: Have you got your cigarettes and matches, Fred?

MR BROOK: Yes. Have you got your ticket?

MR BROWN: Yes, and I've got a newspaper too. I bought one outside the station.

MR BROOK: The porter's closing the gate. We're late. Hurry up!

Answer these questions:

1 How many men and women are there in the picture on page 49?
2 What did Mr Brook buy from the girl at the station?
3 How many did he buy?
4 How many bags is the porter carrying?
5 What is the woman in black carrying in her hand?
6 Where is she going?
7 How many porters are there in the picture on page 49?
8 What is the man at the gate doing?
9 Where is Mr Brown getting his ticket?
10 What is the porter on the platform doing?

New Words

a booking-clerk ('bukiŋklɑːk)
a booking-office ('bukiŋɔfis)
a box, boxes (bɔks, 'bɔksiz)
  luggage ('lʌgidʒ)
  madam ('mædəm)
a match, matches (mætʃ, 'mætʃiz)
  men (men)
a packet ('pækit)
  people ('piːpl)
a platform ('plætfɔːm)
a porter ('pɔːtə)
a railway ('reilwei)
  sir (səː)
a station ('steiʃn)
a ticket ('tikit)
a train (trein)
an umbrella (ʌm'brelə)
  women ('wimin)
  Fred Brook ('fred 'bruk)

to bring (briŋ)
  brought (brɔːt)
to buy (bai)
  bought (bɔːt)
to carry ('kæri)
  carried ('kærid)
to close (klouz)
  closed (klouzd)
to come (kʌm)
  came (keim)
to drive (draiv)
  drove (drouv)
to get (get)
  got (gɔt)
to go (gou)
  went (went)
to hurry ('hʌri)
  hurried ('hʌrid)
to leave (liːv)
  left (left)

to open ('oupən)
  opened ('oupənd)
to run (rʌn)
  ran (ræn)
to see (siː)
  saw (sɔː)
to sell (sel)
  sold (sould)
to take (teik)
  took (tuk)

black (blæk)
large (lɑːdʒ)
late (leit)
return (ri'təːn)
single ('siŋgl)
small (smɔːl)
some (sʌm)
white (wait)

by (bai)
inside (in'said)
of (ɔv, əv)
outside (aut'said)
through (θruː)

1 one (wʌn)
2 two (tuː)
3 three (θriː)
4 four (fɔː)
5 five (faiv)
6 six (siks)
7 seven ('sevn)
8 eight (eit)
9 nine (nain)
10 ten (ten)
11 eleven (i'levn)
20 twenty ('twenti)

by car (bai 'kɑː)

Sentence Patterns

19 How many?

How many books have I got in my hand?
How many cigarettes did he buy?
How many bags is the porter carrying?
How many people are there in this picture?

20 There is, there are

There is a table in this room.
There is a dog under the table.
There are three pictures on the wall of this room.
There are seven people in this picture.

Is there a man in the room?
Is there a dog under that table?
How many books are there on that table?
Are there seven or eight people in this picture?

21 (*a*) Simple Past tense

Mr Brown is walking across the platform.
He walked across the platform.

The porter is closing the door.
He closed the door.

The policeman is stopping the cars.
He stopped the cars.

David is opening the window.
He opened the window.

(*b*) Mr Brown is taking his bag from the car.
He took his bag from the car.

Mr Brook is going to London.
He went to London.

Tom is driving to the station.
He drove to the station.

Susan is buying a hat and coat.
She bought a hat and coat.

Mrs Brown is speaking to the postman.
She spoke to the postman.

(c) What did Mr Brown buy at the station?
He bought a ticket to London.

What did Mr Brook buy from the girl?
He bought some cigarettes and some matches.

What did the porter do?
He carried the woman's luggage to the train.

Where did Mr Brown leave his car?
He left it at the station.

Where did Mr Brown see his friend?
He saw him in the street.

Exercises

A. Put the right word into these sentences:

Example: Mr Brown ... his car at the station.
Mr Brown left his car at the station.

1 The porter ... the doors of the train.
2 The room was warm: Mrs Brown ... a window.
3 Susan ... with Tom to the shops.
4 David ... a bag to the train.
5 Tom ... his car into the town.
6 The policeman ... the cars in the street.
7 Mr Brook ... a packet of cigarettes.
8 Mr Brown ... to the booking-clerk.
9 Tom ... his friend in the street.
10 Susan ... to London yesterday.

B. Answer these questions:

1 How many wheels are there on a car?
2 How many hands have you got?
3 How many fingers have you got on one hand?

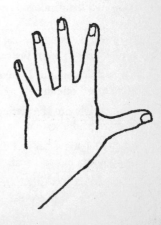

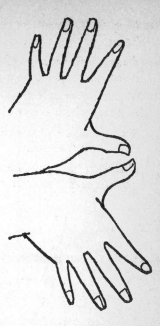

4 How many fingers have you got on two
hands?

5 How many books are there on this table?

6 How many people are there in Mr Brown's house?
7 How many cigarettes is Mr Brook buying at the
station?
8 How many eggs are there on this plate?

9 How many matches are there in this box?

finger ('fiŋgə)
wheel (wiːl)

55

C. Look at this picture. Make six sentences with *there is, there are.*

Example: *There is a door in this room.*

D. What are these people doing in the picture on page 49?

1 Mr Brown
2 Mr Brook
3 the porter
4 the booking-clerk
5 the woman in the black coat
6 the man at the gate
7 the men and women on the platform
8 the porter on the platform

Unit 7

Taxi!

Yesterday Mr Brown went to London by train with his friend Mr Fred Brook. They got out at Victoria Station. Mr Brown was late; he didn't walk from the station to his office, but took a taxi.

His taxi came round a corner near the Houses of Parliament and a car ran into it. Some windows broke and a wheel of the taxi came off. Mr Brown fell and hit his head on the door. The car did not stop; it drove away. A policeman shouted to the driver, but the car did not stop.

Mr Brown got out of the taxi. The policeman spoke to Mr Brown and to the taxi-driver; he was very angry. He wrote the number of the car in his little black book; the number was XYZ 123. The taxi-driver was angry too; he shouted and waved his arms.

The policeman asked a lot of questions. Then Mr Brown walked to his office. He is the manager of a bank. There he sat on a chair and drank a cup of tea. He did not work that morning.

MR BROOK:	Here we are at Victoria.
MR BROWN:	Yes. I'm late. I didn't get up early this morning. Good-bye, Fred. Is there a taxi? Yes, there are some there. Taxi!
TAXI-DRIVER:	Where to, sir?
MR BROWN:	The Strand. London Bank. I'm late. Hurry, please!
TAXI-DRIVER:	All right, sir.

TAXI-DRIVER:	He came round that corner, and he ran into my taxi. He didn't stop.
POLICEMAN:	Did you get his number?
TAXI-DRIVER:	Yes, I got the number: XYZ 123.
POLICEMAN:	Good. Did you see the driver?
TAXI-DRIVER:	Yes. He was a tall man with black hair. He had a blue coat, but he hadn't a hat.

MR BROWN:	I'm late. My office is in the Strand. The London Bank. I'm the manager.
POLICEMAN:	What is your name, sir, please?
MR BROWN:	Brown, John Brown.
POLICEMAN:	Thank you, sir. Are you hurt?
MR BROWN:	No. I only hit my head on the door of the taxi.
POLICEMAN:	Did you see the number of the car, sir?
MR BROWN:	No, I didn't.
POLICEMAN:	Did you see the driver?
MR BROWN:	No, I didn't see him. He came round the corner and ran into the taxi. I didn't see his face.
POLICEMAN:	All right, sir. Did you say the London Bank?
MR BROWN:	Yes. In the Strand. I'm the manager.
POLICEMAN:	Thank you, sir.
MR BROWN:	Is there a telephone near here?
POLICEMAN:	Yes. On the corner of that street.

MR BROWN:	A cup of tea, please.
CLERK:	Are you all right, sir?
MR BROWN:	Yes, thank you. A car came round the corner and hit my taxi. It took a wheel

off the taxi. I fell and hit my head.

CLERK: Did the driver of the car stop?

MR BROWN: No, he didn't. But the policeman got his number.

Answer these questions:

1 Where did Mr Brown go yesterday?
2 Where did he get out of the train?
3 What did the car do to Mr Brown's taxi?
4 What came off the taxi?
5 What broke?
6 What did the policeman do?
7 Did Mr Brown see the driver's face?
8 Did the taxi-driver see the driver of the car?
9 Was the driver tall or short?
10 What did Mr Brown have in his room at the bank?

New Words

an arm (ɑːm)
a bank (bæŋk)
a corner ('kɔːnə)
a driver ('draivə)
a face (feis)
 hair (hɛə)
a head (hed)
a lot (lɔt)
a manager ('mænidʒə)
a number ('nʌmbə)
an office ('ɔfis)
a question ('kwestʃn)
a taxi ('tæksi)
 tea (tiː)
a telephone ('telifoun)
 Parliament ('pɑːləmənt)

the Strand (ðə 'strænd)
 Victoria (vik'tɔːriə)

to ask (ɑːsk)
 asked (ɑːskt)
to break (breik)
 broke (brouk)
to fall (fɔːl)
 fell (fel)
to hit (hit)
 hit (hit)
to shout (ʃaut)
 shouted ('ʃautid)
to work (wəːk)
 worked (wəːkt)
to write (rait)
 wrote (rout)

angry ('æŋgri)
blue (bluː)
early ('əːli)
hurt (həːt)

away (ə'wei)
off (ɔf)
only ('ounli)

round (raund)
then (ðen)

by taxi (bai 'tæksi)
by train (bai 'trein)
Here we are! (hiə wi 'aː)
to get out (tə 'get 'aut)
to get up (tə 'get 'ʌp)
to run into (tə 'rʌn 'intə)

Sentence Patterns

22 'A', 'an'—'some'

The porter is carrying a bag.
He is carrying some bags.

Mr Brook is buying a newspaper.
He is buying some newspapers.

Mr Brown has a match.
He has some matches.

There is an egg on that table.
There are some eggs on that table.

There was a girl in the room.
There were some girls in the room.

23 Simple Past tense—Negative

(a) Regular verbs

Mr Brown walked to the office.
Mr Brown did not (didn't) walk to the office.

The policeman shouted to the driver.
The policeman did not (didn't) shout to the driver.

Mr Brook hurried to the train.
Mr Brook did not (didn't) hurry to the train.

The porter closed the doors.
The porter did not (didn't) close the doors.

(b) Irregular verbs

The driver got the number of the car.
The driver did not (didn't) get the number of the car.

He came here yesterday.
He did not (didn't) come here yesterday.

Mr Brown took a taxi.
He did not (didn't) take a taxi.

They went to the office.
They did not (didn't) go to the office.

He stood near the gate.
He did not (didn't) stand near the gate.

Mr Brown saw the driver.
He did not (didn't) see the driver.

24   Simple Past tense—Questions

Did Mr Brown walk to the station?	Yes, he did. No, he didn't.
Did the porter close the doors?	Yes, he did. No, he didn't.
Did the woman shout to the driver?	Yes, she did. No, she didn't.
Did you speak to the policeman, Mr Brown?	Yes, I did. No, I didn't.
Did the driver see the car's number?	Yes, he did. No, he didn't.
Did the car come round the corner?	Yes, it did. No, it didn't.
Did Mr Brown and Mr Brook take a taxi?	Yes, they did. No, they didn't.

Exercises

A. Put the right words into these sentences:

Mr Brown (*go, went, going*) to London yesterday. Did he (*drive, drove, driving*) or did he (*walked, walking, walk*)? He (*take, taking, took*) a taxi from the station to his office. Did a car (*ran, run, running*) into his taxi? Yes, it (*come, coming, came*) round a corner and (*run, ran, running*) into his taxi. There (*is, was*) a policeman in the street. Did he (*shouting, shouted, shout*) at the driver? Yes, and he (*wrote, write, writing*) the number of the car in his book. Mr Brown didn't (*saw, see, seeing*) the driver. In his office he (*sit, sitting, sat*) down on a chair and (*has, had, having*) a cup of tea.

B. *Put this into the Simple Past tense:*

Mr Brown is coming out of the station. He is saying good-bye to Mr Brook. He is taking a taxi to his office. The taxi is driving down the street. A car is coming round a corner. It is running into the taxi. The taxi-driver is shouting at the driver of the car and waving his arms. He is speaking to a policeman. The policeman is writing the number of the car in his book. Mr Brown is late and he is angry.

C. *Make negative sentences with these words:*

Example: Mrs Brown, eating, breakfast
Mrs Brown isn't eating her breakfast.

1　we, London, yesterday
2　car, run into, taxi
3　driver, car, stop
4　taxi, station
5　Mr Brown, get up, early
6　Mr Brook, London, train
7　Tom and Susan, see, friend, town
8　Mr Brown, letter, this morning
9　dog, picture, page 57
10　David, break, window

D. *Look at the picture on page 57. Write six sentences about this picture with a plural noun in each sentence.*

Unit 8

The Barbecue

This evening Susan and David with Susan's boy-friend, Tom Smith, are going to have a barbecue in their garden. Many of their friends are going to be there, and they are going to have a very happy evening. It is summer, and a very warm day.

The Browns have a big garden round their house. In it there are some tall trees and many flowers. This evening Mr and Mrs Brown are not at home; they are with some friends, and the young people are having a barbecue. This morning Susan went to town and bought steaks and bacon and sausages for the barbecue. This afternoon David made a fire in the garden and put some iron bars over it. Susan got everything ready, and Tom brought some wine and beer. Now all their friends are here and the barbecue is going to start.

Tom is the cook; he is a very good cook. Susan brought the steaks and bacon and sausages to Tom and he put them on the iron bars. David made a big fire under the bars. Now their friends are sitting on the grass or at little tables, eating—and eating! They are all very hungry.

But Susan is looking at the sky. The sky is very black; they are going to have some rain. Now the rain is coming down fast. They are all running into the house. The rain is putting out the fire. That is the end of the barbecue.

MRS BROWN: Are you ready for the barbecue, Susan?
SUSAN: Yes, thank you, Mother.
MRS BROWN: Have a good evening, and don't burn the sausages!
SUSAN: No, that's all right. Tom is going to be the cook.
MR BROWN: And don't burn the trees.
DAVID: *No*, Father.

DAVID: Who's going to be the cook?
SUSAN: Tom is.
TOM: Right. Now I'm going to begin. Make a big fire, David.
DAVID: There *is* a big fire.
TOM: Good. Susan, bring the steaks, please. Put the sausages into that pan.
SUSAN: How many?
TOM: Twenty. Now put some bacon into this pan, David.
DAVID: Who *is* the cook? We're doing all the work.
TOM: No, you aren't. Be careful. You're burning that bacon.

SUSAN: They're all here now. We're going to eat.
TOM: Come and get it. Bring your plates. Steaks, sausages, bacon. Be careful! It's all very hot.
JIM BLAKE: A steak, please. And some sausages. I'm hungry.
DAVID: Beer or wine, Jim?
JIM: Beer, please. I'm going to enjoy this.
TOM: Come on, Susan. You haven't got anything. What are you going to have?
SUSAN: One sausage and a piece of bacon.
DAVID: Some wine?
SUSAN: Yes, please.

SUSAN: The sky's very black. We're going to have some rain.

DAVID: It *is* raining. We're all going to get wet.

TOM: Run into the house. David, bring those sausages.

JIM: Thank you. It was a very nice barbecue. We all enjoyed it.

DAVID: What are we going to do now?

SUSAN: We're going to dance. I'm going to put my new records on the record-player. Come on!

Answer these questions:

1 Where are Mr and Mrs Brown going to be this evening?
2 What are David, Susan and Tom going to do this evening?
3 What did Mr Brown say to the young people? He said, '...
4 What are the young people going to cook?
5 Where are they going to cook?
6 What are they going to drink?
7 Where are the young people going to eat?
8 What is David going to do?
9 It began to rain. Where did the young people run?
10 What did the young people do then?

New Words

an afternoon ('ɑːftə'nuːn)
anything ('eniθiŋ)
a bar (bɑː)
a barbecue ('bɑːbikjuː)
beer (biə)
a cook (kuk)
a day (dei)
an end (end)
an evening ('iːvniŋ)
everything ('evriθiŋ)
a flower ('flauə)
a garden ('gɑːdn)
grass (grɑːs)
iron ('aiən)
a pan (pæn)

rain (rein)
a record ('rekɔːd)
a record-player ('rekɔːd 'pleiə)
a sausage ('sɔsidʒ)
the sky (skai)
a steak (steik)
the summer ('sʌmə)
a tree (triː)
wine (wain)

to begin (bi'gin)
began (bi'gæn)
to burn (bəːn)
burned (bəːnd)
to cook (kuk)
cooked (kukt)

to dance (dɑːns)
    danced (dɑːnst)
to enjoy (in'dʒɔi)
    enjoyed (in'dʒɔid)
to look (luk)
    looked (lukt)
to make (meik)
    made (meid)

to rain (rein)
    rained (reind)

to start (stɑːt)
    started ('stɑːtid)
hot (hɔt)
many ('meni)
nice (nais)
ready ('redi)
young (jʌŋ)

Sentence Patterns

25 (a) Future tense with 'going to'

David He Susan She	is 's		make a fire. cook some sausages. have breakfast.
I	am 'm	going to	
Susan and David We You They	are 're		enjoy a happy evening. get wet.

(b) Future tense with 'going to'—Negative

David He Susan She	is not isn't		cook the steaks. burn the sausages. drink beer. be at home this evening. dance.
I	am not 'm not	going to	
Mr and Mrs Brown We You They	are not aren't		

(c)   **Future tense with 'going to'—Questions**

Is	Tom he Susan she		make a fire? cook the steaks?
Am	I	going to	be late for breakfast?
Are	Susan and David we you they		enjoy the evening? have a barbecue?

Exercises

A. Put the right verb into these sentences:

1 Tomorrow Susan and David (*had, are having, are going to have*) a barbecue.
2 Did David (*made, make, making*) a big fire?
3 Is Tom (*cooking, cooks, cooked*) the steaks?
4 Susan, (*putting, puts, put*) those steaks in the pan, please.
5 Tom did not (*brought, bringing, bring*) beer to the barbecue.
6 Are the Browns (*coming, came, come*) home late this evening?
7 The young people are going to (*having, had, have*) a barbecue.
8 Don't (*drink, drinking, drank*) all that beer, David.
9 Mr Brown (*is, was, are*) not going to London today.

B. Make plural sentences with these words:

1 boy, cooking, sausage
2 boy, putting, steak, plate
3 girl, drinking, wine
4 tree, this, garden
5 good, cook, burn, bacon
6 man, go, office, today
7 woman, buy, hat, coat
8 he, put, knife, fork, table

C. Make sentences in the Simple Past tense from these words:

Example: my brother, break, window, yesterday
My brother broke that window yesterday.

1 Susan, buy, bread, cakes
2 Tom, take, friends, station
3 Mrs Brown, go, shops, morning
4 David, drive, fast, town
5 policeman, speak, driver, car
6 Jim Blake, come, barbecue, girl-friend
7 all the people, run, house
8 Mr Brown, leave, car, station

D. Make sentences in the Imperative from these words:

1 put, bacon, pan
2 light, fire, garden
3 not burn, trees, garden
4 not drive, fast, town
5 leave, car, house
6 not sit, wet, grass
7 careful, not break, record-player
8 bring, flowers, garden, Susan
9 give, dog, breakfast, David
10 not run, street, car
wet (wet)

Unit 9

He Asked Questions

The Browns are having dinner; it is seven o'clock in the evening. Mr Brown went to London by train at nine o'clock this morning and came home at six o'clock this evening. Tom Smith is having dinner with the Browns; he is sitting next to Susan. Tom is tall and good-looking.

MRS BROWN: You aren't eating, Tom. Have some cheese. It's very nice.

TOM: No, thank you, Mrs Brown. The dinner was very good. You're a good cook.

MRS BROWN: Thank you, Tom. And you're a very nice boy.

MR BROWN: Some wine, Tom. Your glass is empty.

TOM: Thank you. A little, please.

MRS BROWN: A man came to the house this morning, John, and asked me a lot of questions.

MR BROWN: What questions?

MRS BROWN: How many rooms we have. How many people there are in the house.

DAVID: And did you tell him?

MRS BROWN: Yes. It was twelve o'clock, and I was very busy. I answered his questions, and

he wrote it all down in a book. Then
he went away.

SUSAN: Why did he come to the house?

TOM: Perhaps he was from the Town Hall.

MRS BROWN: Perhaps he was.

MR BROWN: What are we going to do tomorrow?

SUSAN: We're going to drive to the sea. Don't
go to work tomorrow, Tom. Come to
the sea with us.

TOM: All right.

MRS BROWN: Are we going to take the dog with us?

DAVID: Yes, he's good in the car.

MRS BROWN: Where are you two going this evening?

SUSAN: To a dance in town with Jim Blake and
his new girl-friend. We don't know her.
We're going to meet them at nine
o'clock.

MR BROWN: Don't come home very late. We're going
to leave the house at ten o'clock in the
morning.

Tom and Susan enjoyed the dance, and he brought her home at one
o'clock. Mr and Mrs Brown were in bed, and the house was very
quiet. Tom opened the door with Susan's key.

SUSAN: Come in and say good-night. Be very quiet.
They're all in bed.

TOM: No, they aren't. Look, there's a light under
the dining-room door.

SUSAN: Who is it? It's one o'clock in the morning.

TOM: I'm going to see.

SUSAN: Be careful. Perhaps it's a thief.

Tom walked to the dining-room door.
Then the door opened, and a man came out.
He carried a bag in his hand. He saw Tom and
Susan and began to run to the front door.

SUSAN: It *is* a thief. Stop him, Tom!

Tom put out his foot and the man fell. Tom sat on him. The bag opened and all the things inside fell out.

SUSAN: Look, all our things. He had them in his bag.
TOM: Telephone for the police, Susan.

Then Mr and Mrs Brown came downstairs.

MR BROWN: What's the matter, Tom? Who's that man, and what's he doing there?
TOM: He's a thief. We found him in the dining-room. He had your things in that bag.
MRS BROWN: That's the man. I told you about him at dinner. He came to the house this morning and asked me all those questions.
TOM: *He's* not going to ask more questions. The police are going to ask the questions. And here they are!

Answer these questions:

1 A man came to Mrs Brown's house. Was he from the Town Hall?
2 What did he do?
3 At what time did he come?
4 What time did Mr Brown go to work in the morning?
5 What time did he come home?

6 What are the Browns going to do the next morning?
7 Where did Tom and Susan go that evening?
8 What time did they come home?
9 Who did they find in the house?
10 Where was he?
11 How did Tom stop him?
12 What was in his bag?

New Words

cheese (tʃiːz)
a dance (dɑːns)
dinner ('dinə)
a foot, feet (fut, fiːt)
a girl-friend ('gəːlfrend)
a glass (glɑːs)
a key (kiː)
a light (lait)
the matter ('mætə)
a night (nait)
the police (pə'liːs)
the sea (siː)
a thief, thieves (θiːf, θiːvz)
a thing (θiŋ)
a town hall ('taun 'hɔːl)
work (wəːk)

to answer ('ɑːnsə)
answered ('ɑːnsəd)
to find (faind)
found (faund)
to meet (miːt)
met (met)
to telephone ('telifoun)
telephoned ('telifound)
to tell (tel)
told (tould)
busy ('bizi)
empty ('empti)

good-looking ('gud'lukiŋ)
quiet ('kwaiət)

me (miː, mi)
him (him)
her² (həː)
us (ʌs)

about (ə'baut)
downstairs ('daun'stɛəz)
more (mɔː)
next (nekst)
o'clock (ə'klɔk)
perhaps (pə'hæps)
tomorrow (tə'mɔrou)
why? (wai)
good night (gud'nait)
a lot of (ə 'lɔt əv)
what's the matter? ('wɔts ðə 'mætə)

12 twelve (twelv)
13 thirteen ('θəː'tiːn)
14 fourteen ('fɔː'tiːn)
15 fifteen 'fif'tiːn)
16 sixteen ('siks'tiːn)
17 seventeen ('sevn'tiːn)
18 eighteen ('ei'tiːn)
19 nineteen ('nain'tiːn)
20 twenty ('twenti)
21 twenty-one ('twenti 'wʌn)

Sentence Patterns

26 Personal pronouns—objective

Before a verb: I, he, she, it, we, you, they
After a verb or preposition: me, him, her, it, us, you, them

(a) *Before and after a verb*

TOM saw *his friend*	HE saw *him.*
HIS FRIEND saw *Tom.*	HE saw *him.*
TOM told *Susan.*	HE told *her.*
SUSAN met *Tom.*	SHE met *him.*
THE THIEF hit *me.*	HE hit *me.*
I hit *the thief.*	I hit *him.*
WE met *our friends.*	WE met *them.*
OUR FRIENDS met *us.*	THEY met *us.*
THE POLICE asked *the Browns* some questions.	THEY asked *them* some questions.
THE BROWNS asked *the police* some questions.	THEY asked *them* some questions.
YOU left *your friends* at the station.	YOU left *them* at the station.
YOUR FRIENDS left *you* at the station.	THEY left *you* at the station.

(b) *After a preposition*

Mr Brown gave the book to *me.*
Susan saw the postman and took a letter from *him.*
We met our friends and they sat near *us* in the train.
She stood near the wall and the picture fell on *her.*
Will you take Susan with *you* to the shops?
The policeman stopped the car in front of *us.*
She looked at *him* but she didn't say a word.
There are some letters for *them* on the table.

27 Time—hours

What's the time, please?

It's one o'clock.	1 A.M. or 1 P.M.*
It's two o'clock.	2 A.M. or 2 P.M.
It's three o'clock.	3 A.M. or 3 P.M.
It's four o'clock.	4 A.M. or 4 P.M.
It's five o'clock.	5 A.M. or 5 P.M.
It's six o'clock.	6 A.M. or 6 P.M.
It's seven o'clock.	7 A.M. or 7 P.M.
It's eight o'clock.	8 A.M. or 8 P.M.
It's nine o'clock.	9 A.M. or 9 P.M.
It's ten o'clock.	10 A.M. or 10 P.M.
It's eleven o'clock.	11 A.M. or 11 P.M.
It's twelve o'clock.	12 noon or 12 midnight

* A.M. = *ante meridiem* (Latin) before noon.
P.M. = *post meridiem* (Latin) after noon.

Times in Railway Timetables

It's one o'clock in the morning.	01.00
It's six o'clock in the morning.	06.00
It's nine o'clock in the morning.	09.00
It's twelve o'clock midday.	12.00
It's three o'clock in the afternoon.	15.00
It's six o'clock in the evening.	18.00
It's nine o'clock in the evening.	21.00
It's eleven o'clock at night.	23.00
It's twelve o'clock midnight.	24.00

Exercises

A. Put the right pronoun into these sentences:

1 Tom took Susan with ... to a dance.
2 Susan's boy-friend is sitting next to ...
3 'The man asked ... a lot of questions,' Mrs Brown told her husband, 'but I didn't answer ...'
4 We saw Jim Blake, but ... didn't see ...
5 You've got my book. Who gave ... to ...?

6 The thief ran to the door, but Tom stopped ...
7 We met our friends and took ... to a dance.
8 The thief fell, and Tom sat on ...
9 Are you coming with ... to the barbecue?
10 The book fell on ..., but she wasn't hurt.

B. (a)

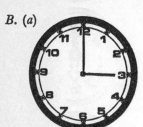

P.M.

It's three o'clock in the afternoon.

What time is it?

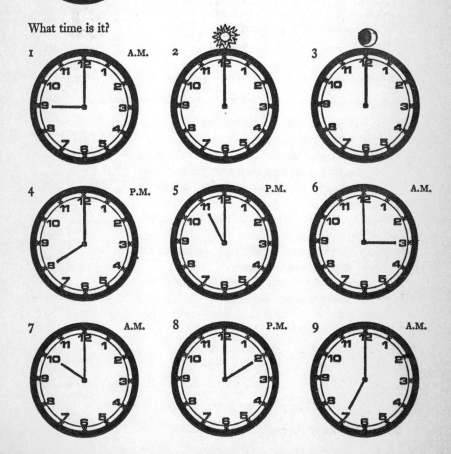

1 A.M.   2   3

4 P.M.   5 P.M.   6 A.M.

7 A.M.   8 P.M.   9 A.M.

IO   P.M.

(*b*) 8 A.M. *It's eight o'clock in the morning.*

What time is it?

1	10 A.M.	2	3 P.M.
3	9 P.M.	4	1 A.M.
5	11 P.M.	6	21.00 hours
7	15.00 hours	8	17.00 hours
9	10.00 hours	10	19.00 hours

C. *Put the past tense form of the verb in brackets into these sentences:*

A thief (*go*) into a hat shop, and his friend (*stand*) out-side. The thief (*have*) an old hat on his head.
'A new hat, please,' he (*say*) to the man in the shop, and he (*put*) his old hat on a chair near the door. The man in the shop (*give*) him a new hat, and he (*put*) it on his head.
'This hat is nice,' the thief (*say*). 'How much is it?'

Then his friend (*come*) into the shop, (*take*) the old hat from the chair, and (*run*) away.
'Stop him!' (*shout*) the thief, and (*run*) out of the shop, with the new hat on his head.
The man in the shop (*stand*) at his door—but the two thieves (*not come*) back!

back (bæk)

D. Tom Smith said, 'The police are going to ask the questions'.

Write down some of the questions.

Unit 10

Mrs Brown Goes Shopping

The Browns live in Bishopton. Bishopton is a small town thirty miles from London. Mr Brown works in London; he goes there on Monday, Tuesday, Wednesday, Thursday and Friday. He doesn't work on Saturday or Sunday. Their son, David, is seventeen years old; his age is seventeen. He goes to school. Their daughter, Susan, is nineteen; she works in an office. Her boy-friend, Tom Smith, is twenty; he works in a factory. He is going to be a factory manager one day.

Today is Monday. Mrs Brown always goes shopping on Monday afternoon. She sometimes goes on Wednesday and Friday. She doesn't go shopping on Thursday; the shops close on Thursday afternoons. She often meets her friend, Mrs Morton, in Bishopton.

Mrs Brown is shopping in Bishopton now. She is buying some cakes and bread at the baker's. Near the baker's shop is the greengrocer's. He sells fruit and vegetables: apples, oranges, pears, cabbages, onions and potatoes. Mr Stephens, the baker, is always polite to his customers. 'The customer is always right,' he says. But his cakes are not always fresh and his bread is sometimes dry.

Mr Jones, the greengrocer, is not always polite and sometimes he gives the wrong change. But his fruit and vegetables are always fresh and his shop is very clean.

Bishopton is a busy little town. There are always a lot of buses, cars, motor-cycles and bicycles in the street. Outside the baker's shop in the picture there is a van; the driver takes bread and cakes to the houses in and near the town every day.

MRS BROWN *(at the baker's)*: Good afternoon, Mr Stephens. I want two white loaves and one brown loaf, please. Your van-driver didn't bring the bread this morning.

BAKER: I'm very sorry, Mrs Brown. He's a new driver. He doesn't know all the houses, and he sometimes forgets. Are you going to take the bread with you?

MRS BROWN: Yes, please. It's for tea today. What cakes have you got?

BAKER: The cakes in the window are nice.

MRS BROWN: Are they fresh? Do you make your cakes every morning?

BAKER: Yes, madam. So they're always fresh.

MRS BROWN: One large cake and twelve small cakes, please. How much is that?

BAKER: The large cake is twenty-five pence, and

the small cakes are five pence each. That
makes eighty-five pence.

MRS BROWN: Thank you. Here's a pound.

BAKER: Thank you, Mrs Brown. Fifteen pence
change. Good afternoon.

MRS MORTON (*at the greengrocer's*): How much are
the oranges, Mr Jones?

GREENGROCER: Three pence each, madam. Five for
ten pence. They're very sweet.

MRS MORTON: Five, please. How much are the apples?

GREENGROCER: Ten pence a pound the eating apples,
and eight pence a pound the cooking
apples.

MRS MORTON: Two pounds of eating apples, please,
and one pound of cooking apples.

GREENGROCER: Is that all, madam?

MRS MORTON: Yes, thank you.

GREENGROCER: Thirty-eight pence, please.

MRS MORTON: Oh, yes. A cabbage and two pounds of
onions, please.

GREENGROCER: That's eighteen pence, and thirty-
eight pence makes fifty-six. Fifty-six
from one pound. Forty-four pence
change. Thank you, madam.

MRS MORTON: Put them in this bag, please.

(MRS MORTON *meets* MRS BROWN *in the street*)

MRS MORTON: Hello, Mary! What a nice day!

MRS BROWN: Hello, Joan. How are you? Are you
shopping?

MRS MORTON: Yes. I wanted some fruit and vegetables,
that's all.

MRS BROWN: Stephens' bread-van didn't bring the
bread this morning, so I came into the
town for it. And some cakes for tea.

MRS MORTON: How's John?

MRS BROWN: Very well, thank you. He's in London
today. Come back and have tea with
me.

MRS MORTON: Thank you. My husband isn't home for tea today.

MRS BROWN: Come on, then! John always leaves the car at the station for me on Monday.

MRS MORTON: Does he walk home from the station?

MRS BROWN: No, he comes by bus.

MRS MORTON: When does John come home in the evening?

MRS BROWN: About six o'clock.

Answer these questions:

1 Why doesn't Mrs Brown go shopping on Thursday?
2 What does a greengrocer sell?
3 How old is Susan's brother?
4 What does a baker's van-driver do?
5 How much did Mrs Brown give the baker?
6 How much did Mrs Morton give the greengrocer for fruit?
7 Where does Mr Brown leave his car on Monday?
8 Where does David go every day?
9 Where do the Browns live?
10 How much does an orange cost?
11 How much do apples cost?

New Words

age (eidʒ)
an apple ('æpl)
a baker ('beikə)
a bicycle ('baisikl)
a bus (bʌs)
a cabbage ('kæbidʒ)
change (tʃeindʒ)
a customer ('kʌstəmə)
a factory ('fæktri)
fruit (fruːt)
a greengrocer ('griːngrousə)
a loaf, loaves (louf, louvz)
a mile (mail)
money ('mʌni)

a motor-cycle ('moutəsaikl)
an onion ('ʌnjən)
an orange ('ɔrindʒ)
a pear (pɛə)
a penny ('peni)
pence (pens)
a potato (pə'teitou)
a pound (paund)
a school (skuːl)
shopping ('ʃɔpiŋ)
a van (væn)
a vegetable ('vedʒtəbl)
a week (wiːk)
a year (jiə)

Bishopton ('biʃəptən)
Jones (dʒounz)
Morton ('mɔːtn)
Stephens ('stiːvənz)

brown (braun)
clean (kliːn)
dry (drai)
each (iːtʃ)
every ('evri)
fresh (freʃ)
much (mʌtʃ)
polite (pə'lait)
sweet (swiːt)
wrong (rɔŋ)
how? (hau)
when? (wen)
always ('ɔːlweiz)
often ('ɔfn, 'ɔftn)
sometimes ('sʌmtaimz)

to cost (kɔst)
   cost (kɔst)
to forget (fə'get)
   forgot (fə'gɔt)
to know (nou)
   knew (njuː)
to live (liv)
   lived (livd)
to want (wɔnt)
   wanted ('wɔntid)

Sunday ('sʌndi)
Monday ('mʌndi)
Tuesday ('tjuːzdi)
Wednesday ('wenzdi)
Thursday ('θəːzdi)
Friday ('fraidi)
Saturday ('sætədi)

30 thirty ('θəːti)
40 forty ('fɔːti)
50 fifty ('fifti)
60 sixty ('siksti)
70 seventy ('sevnti)
80 eighty ('eiti)
90 ninety ('nainti)
100 a hundred (ə 'hʌndrəd)

Sentence Patterns

28 (a) Simple Present tense

The Browns live in Bishopton.
These shops close on Thursday.
We go to London every morning.
I meet him at the station every day.

Mr Brown works in London.
He goes there every day.
The baker sells bread and cakes.

Mrs Brown always goes shopping on Monday.
She often meets her friend in Bishopton.
Mr Jones sometimes gives the wrong change.

Simple Present tense	*Present Continuous tense*
Mrs Brown goes shopping on Monday.	She is shopping in Bishopton now.
Porters carry bags at the station.	This porter is carrying a bag to the train.
Mr Brown drives to London every day.	He is driving to London now.
Mr Stephens sells potatoes.	He is selling some potatoes to Mrs Morton.
The Browns have breakfast in their dining-room.	Today they are having breakfast in the garden.

(b) Simple Present tense—Negative

The Browns don't live in London.
Bakers don't sell apples.
They don't sit at home on Saturday.
We don't buy cakes at the greengrocer's.
I don't live in Bishopton.

Mr Brown doesn't go to London on Saturday.
Tom Smith doesn't work on Sunday.
Susan doesn't eat much breakfast.

Mrs Brown doesn't often go shopping on Saturday.
Mr Jones doesn't always give the right change.

(c) Simple Present tense—Questions

Do these shops close on Thursday?	Yes, they do.
Do the Browns live in London?	Yes, they do.
Do you make your cakes every day?	Yes, I do.
Do they work on Saturday?	No, they don't.

Does Tom work in a factory?	Yes, he does.
Does Susan begin work at nine o'clock?	Yes, she does.
Does Mr Brown drive to London every day?	No, he doesn't.

When do you go shopping, Mrs Brown?
When do the shops close in Bishopton?
When does Mr Brown leave home in the morning?
When does he begin work?

29 How old?

How old is David Brown?	He's seventeen years old.
What is his age?	He's seventeen.
	Seventeen.
How old is Susan Brown?	She's nineteen years old.
What is her age?	She's nineteen.
	Nineteen.
How old is this house?	It's fifteen years old.
	Fifteen years.

30 How much?

How much does an orange cost?	An orange costs three pence.
How much do oranges cost?	Oranges cost three pence each.
How much is an orange?	Three pence.
How much are oranges?	Three pence each.
How much does a pound of apples cost?	A pound of apples cost ten pence.
How much do apples cost?	Apples cost ten pence a pound.
How much is a pound of apples?	Ten pence.
How much are apples?	Ten pence a pound.

Exercises

A. Make negative sentences in the Simple Present tense with these words:

1 David, go, school, every day
2 Mr Stephens, give, wrong change
3 Tom, Susan, dancing
4 the baker, make, cakes, every day
5 Browns, have, dinner, sitting-room
6 Tom, begin, work, seven o'clock
7 we, write, friends, every week
8 Mrs Brown, go, shopping, Thursday
9 Mr Brown, buy, new car, every year

B.   This is Peter:

Write what Peter does every day,
and at what time he does it.

84

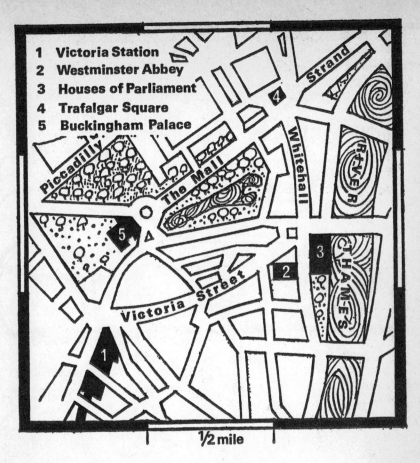

1 **Victoria Station**
2 **Westminster Abbey**
3 **Houses of Parliament**
4 **Trafalgar Square**
5 **Buckingham Palace**

½ mile

C. Put these words into the right places in this passage:
by, to, at, in, across, with, along, round, off, near, inside

Yesterday I went ... London ... my friend Joan. We went ... train.
... Victoria Station we left the train and took a bus ... Victoria Street ...
Westminster Abbey. We got ... the bus ... the Abbey and went ... We
walked ... the Abbey, then we went ... the street ... the Houses of Parlia-
ment; they are ... the Abbey. Then we had some coffee ... a shop ... the
Strand.

D. *Look at this picture. Then write six questions about the people in the picture.*

Example: *What is the girl carrying in her hand?*

Unit 11

At Susan's Office

Susan Brown works in an office. She is secretary to
Mr Robinson, manager of a factory. In this factory
they make clothes: suits and shirts for men, coats
and skirts for women.

In this picture she is sitting at her desk in the office. On the desk
there are some papers, some flowers and a typewriter. She is typing
a letter for Mr Robinson. At the office Susan wears a dark skirt, a
white blouse and black shoes.

Mr Robinson, the manager, is sitting at his desk in his office. He is
a tall man, wearing a blue suit and a red tie. His hair is brown.

Every morning from Monday to Friday Susan comes to the office at nine o'clock. First she opens Mr Robinson's letters. At ten o'clock Mr Robinson rings the bell on his desk and Susan goes into his office with the letters. Look, Mr Robinson is ringing his bell now. He will read the letters and give Susan the answers to the important letters, and she will write these in her book. She will then go back to her desk and begin to type.

At eleven o'clock she will make some coffee and take a cup to Mr Robinson. He doesn't like any sugar in his coffee. After that she will type letters or do some other work until half past twelve. Sometimes she goes home to lunch and sometimes she has lunch in town with her boy-friend, Tom Smith. This afternoon she will work in the office until five o'clock and then she will go home. She and Tom won't go dancing this evening; they will go to the theatre.

Susan comes to the office a little before nine o'clock, but this morning she was late. She came to the office at a quarter past nine. Mr Robinson did not like this, and Susan was sorry. She won't be late tomorrow.

Every month Mr Robinson goes away for two or three days to Manchester or Cardiff or Leeds. Last month he went to Manchester; next month he'll go to Leeds. Susan looks after the office. She is a good secretary, and Mr Robinson knows it.

MR ROBINSON (*at the door of his office*): Did you hear the bell, Miss Brown?

SUSAN: No, Mr Robinson. It didn't ring.

MR ROBINSON: Perhaps it isn't working. I'll ask the porter. Are my letters there?

SUSAN: Yes, Mr Robinson. I'll bring them in.

MR ROBINSON: You were late this morning, Miss Brown.

SUSAN: Yes, I was. I'm very sorry. Our clock at home was wrong, and my watch stopped in the night. I was dancing

with my boy-friend late last night. I'll
work this afternoon until half past five.

MR ROBINSON: No, don't do that. But don't be late
again tomorrow.

SUSAN: No, Mr Robinson.

MR ROBINSON: How many letters have you got?

SUSAN: Fifteen.

MR ROBINSON: Are any of them important?

SUSAN: Yes, eight are.

MR ROBINSON: I'll read the important ones now. Sit
down, please, and take down the
answers. We'll answer the others this
afternoon.

SUSAN: Very well, Mr Robinson.
(*The telephone rings*)

MR ROBINSON: Answer that, please.

SUSAN: Robinson and Company. Yes. Mr
Robinson is here. Who is speaking,
please? One moment, please. (*To Mr
Robinson*) Jones and Company of
Leeds for you, Mr Robinson.

MR ROBINSON: Thank you. (*Taking the telephone*)
Robinson here. Yes. You'll have nine
dozen? Good. Yes, they're very good.
All our clothes are good. All right.
On Tuesday, yes. Do you want any
men's shirts? Thank you. Good-bye.
(*To Susan*) Jones and Company want
nine dozen women's coats.

SUSAN: Any men's shirts?

MR ROBINSON: Yes, fifteen dozen.

SUSAN: Shall I write to them?

MR ROBINSON: Yes, please. That's all for now. My
wife and I have tickets for the theatre
this evening. Will you and Tom come
with us?

SUSAN: Thank you, Mr Robinson. That's very
kind. I'll telephone Tom now.

MR ROBINSON: We shall be ready at about a quarter
to seven. Now, is there any coffee,
please? I'm thirsty.

Unit 11

Answer these questions:

1. What do they make in Susan's factory?
2. Will Susan be late tomorrow?
3. What time will she get to the office tomorrow?
4. What is the first thing Susan will do at the office tomorrow morning?
5. What will she do at eleven o'clock?
6. Does Mr Robinson take any sugar in his coffee?
7. What will the porter do to the bell on Mr Robinson's desk?
8. What time will Susan leave the office this evening?
9. Where will she and Tom go this evening?
10. Who will they go with?

New Words

a bell (bel)
a blouse (blauz)
clothes (klouðz)
a company ('kʌmpəni)
a desk (desk)
a dozen ('dʌzn)
a half (hɑːf)
a lunch (lʌntʃ)
a moment ('moumənt)
a month (mʌnθ)
paper ('peipə)
a quarter ('kwɔːtə)
a secretary ('sekritri)
a shirt (ʃəːt)
a shoe (ʃuː)
a skirt (skəːt)
sugar ('ʃugə)
a suit (sjuːt)
a theatre ('θiːətə)
a tie (tai)
a typewriter ('taipraitə)
a watch (wɔtʃ)

Leeds (liːdz)
Manchester ('mæntʃestə)
Miss (mis)
Robinson ('rɔbinsən)

to hear (hiə)
heard (həːd)
to like (laik)
liked (laikt)
to ring (riŋ)
rang (ræŋ)
shall (ʃæl)
to type (taip)
typed (taipt)
to wait (weit)
waited ('weited)
to wear (wɛə)
wore (wɔː)
will (wil)
won't (wount)

any ('eni)
dark (dɑːk)
first (fəːst)
important (im'pɔːtənt)
kind (kaind)
last (lɑːst)
other ('ʌðə)
past (pɑːst)

red (red)
thirsty ('θəːsti)

after ('ɑːftə)

again (ə'gein)
before (bi'fɔː)
until (ʌn'til)

Sentence Patterns

31 (a)   Simple Future tense

Susan will take the letters to the manager.
Mr Robinson will give Susan the answers.
She will (She'll) write the answers in her book.
You will (You'll) find your bag in my car.
They will (They'll) have some coffee at eleven o'clock.

I shall (I'll) work until half past five.
We shall (We'll) be ready at a quarter to seven.

(b)   Simple Future tense—Negative

Susan will not (won't) be late tomorrow.
Susan and Tom will not (won't) go dancing this evening.
They will not (won't) answer all the letters today.
You will not (won't) find any flowers in this garden.

I shall not (shan't) be at work tomorrow.
We shall not (shan't) want those coats until Monday.

(c)   Simple Future tense—Questions

Will Tom be in London tomorrow?
Will Mr and Mrs Brown be at home this evening?
Will you have lunch in town today?
Will they go by car or by train?

Shall I put this bag in the car?
Shall we leave our car at the station?

Where shall we go on Saturday?
When will this shop open?
How many shirts will Mr Robinson send to Jones and Company?

32 'Some'—'any'

There are some typewriters in this office.
Are there any typewriters in this office?
No, there aren't any typewriters in this office.

There are some papers on Susan's desk.
Are there any papers on Susan's desk?
No, there aren't any papers on Susan's desk.

She has some letters for the manager.
Has she any letters for him?
No, she hasn't any letters for him.

They want some men's shirts.
Do they want any men's shirts?
No, they don't want any men's shirts.

33 Time—the quarter hours

What time is it, please?
It's one o'clock.

		Railway Timetables
It's a quarter past one. It's one fifteen.	1.15 A.M. or 1.15 P.M.	01.15 or 13.15
It's half past one. It's one thirty.	1.30 A.M. or 1.30 P.M.	01.30 or 13.30
It's a quarter to two. It's one forty-five.	1.45 A.M. or 1.45 P.M.	01.45 or 13.45
It's a quarter past ten. It's ten fifteen.	10.15 A.M. or 10.15 P.M.	10.15 or 22.15
It's half past ten. It's ten thirty.	10.30 A.M. or 10.30 P.M.	10.30 or 22.30
It's a quarter to eleven. It's ten forty-five.	10.45 A.M. or 10.45 P.M.	10.45 or 22.45

34 Prepositions

These are prepositions:

in, into, inside, outside, on, under, near, to, from, up, down, in front of, behind, between, before, after, with, without, through, round, off, among, across

1   He walked *into* the room.

2   He was *in* the room.

3   He walked *out of* the room.

4   The cup fell *off* the table.

5   The car is *inside* the garage.

6   The car is *outside* the garage.

7   The book is *on* the table.

8   The dog is *under* the table.

9   Mr Brown stood *near* the fire.

10   He stood *in front of* the fire.

11 He is going *to* the station.

12 He is coming *from* the station.

13 She went *up* the stairs (upstairs).

14 She came *down* the stairs (downstairs).

51 He was hungry *before* dinner.

16 He was not hungry *after* dinner.

17 The dog stood *between* Susan and David.

18 A van stopped *behind* Mr Brown's car.

19 Mr Brown walked *to* the station *with* his friend.

20 Mr Brook went to work *without* his coat.

94

21 The man walked *through* the gate.

22 The boys ran *across* the street.

23 The dog ran *round* the tree.

24 She was standing *among the trees.*

a garage ('gærɑːʒ, 'gærɪdʒ)   upstairs ('ʌp'stɛəz)

Exercises

A. (*a*) *Susan and Tom are going to have a holiday by the sea. Write sentences in the Simple Future tense saying what they will do.*

Example: *They will have a holiday by the sea.*

1 go by car
2 visit some friends
3 not do any work for a week
4 get up late every morning
5 wear old clothes

(*b*) *Now Susan is telling Mr Robinson what she and Tom will do on their holiday. What did she say?*
Example: *We'll have a holiday by the sea.*

(*c*) *Now say what they did.*
Example: *They had a holiday by the sea.*

a holiday ('hɔlidi)   to visit ('vizit)

B. Put *some* or *any* into this passage:

'Good morning, Mr Jones. I want ... oranges, please. Have you got ... this morning?'

'No, Mrs Morton, I haven't got ... oranges today, but I have got ... very nice pears.'

'Very well. I'll have ... of those, and ... apples, please. Have you ... English apples?'

'No, I'm sorry. We haven't got ... English apples. But these are nice.'

'All right. ... of those, please. Oh, yes, and I want ... flowers. We haven't got ... in our garden at the moment.'

'Is that all?'

'Yes, thank you. Here's a pound. Is there ... change?'

'No. I shall want ... more. It's one pound twenty.'

C. *Write what the boy or girl in the picture is doing. Then tell him or her not to do it.*

Example: *This boy is eating an apple.*

'Don't eat that apple.'

D. Put one of these words into the blanks in this passage:

my, his, her, your, our, their

Mr Morton drove ... car through the town. ... wife was with him.
'Please stop,' she said. 'I left ... gloves in that shop yesterday.'

She got out and went for ... gloves. ... husband sat in ... car. Then a policeman came up.

'Is this ... car?' he asked.
'Yes, this is ... car.'
'Don't leave ... car here,' said the policeman.
'I'm waiting for ... wife; she's in that shop. She's looking for ... gloves. Then we're going to drive back to ... home.'
'I'm sorry, sir. Please drive ... car away.'
'Where do people leave ... cars in this town?'
'Over there, sir, behind those shops.'

E. Put these into question form:

1   Susan works in an office.
2   She comes to the office at nine o'clock.
3   She came to the office at a quarter past nine this morning.
4   Susan's watch stopped last night.
5   Her manager's name is Mr Robinson.
6   Mr Robinson rang his bell at ten o'clock.
7   He was angry with Susan.
8   Susan is typing at her desk now.
9   Mr Robinson is in his room.
10   Susan will have lunch in town today with Tom Smith.

F. Susan is telling Tom what she did at the office today. What does she say?

Unit 12

In the Classroom

Here is a picture of a classroom in David Brown's school. The boys go to school every day from Monday to Friday. They don't go on Saturday or Sunday; these are holidays. In the morning school starts at nine o'clock and finishes at half past twelve. The boys have an hour and a half for lunch; some boys go home for lunch, others have lunch at school. In the afternoon school starts at two o'clock and finishes at four o'clock. The boys usually do some homework in the evening.

On one afternoon each week the boys play games in the field near the school. Many boys play games on Saturday morning too. In autumn, winter and spring they play football, and in summer there is cricket.

In this picture a class is at work in the classroom. This is not David's class; he is seventeen, but these boys are young. It is afternoon. The boys have worked all the morning, then they have had lunch. Now they are back in the classroom, but some of them are not working; they are looking out of the window. The teacher has given them a lesson about Great Britain, and now he is pointing to the map on the wall. They have written the names of some towns in their note-books; and now the teacher is asking them questions. Some of the boys have listened to the lesson, but some of them have not listened.

The boys in the field are wearing white shirts and trousers. They have finished school work for today and are playing cricket.

Now it is four o'clock. The teacher has taken the map from the wall and has put it into the cupboard. The boys have put their books into their desks and have gone home. The classroom will be quiet and empty until tomorrow morning.

TEACHER: This is a map of Great Britain. This is England, this is Scotland, this is Wales. I have told you the names of some large towns in Great Britain. Have you remembered them?

BOYS: Yes, sir.

TEACHER: We shall see. Thompson, come here.

THOMPSON: Yes, sir.

TEACHER: Where is London on the map?

THOMPSON: Here, sir.

TEACHER: Right. Now point to Edinburgh.

THOMPSON: Here.

TEACHER: And Cardiff.

THOMPSON: Here.

TEACHER: Now point to Liverpool.

THOMPSON: Here.

TEACHER: Good, Thompson. Thank you. You've got them all right. Sit down. Now, Barnes, come here. Point on the map to Glasgow.

BARNES: Here, sir.

TEACHER: No, you've got it wrong, my boy.

Glasgow is here. Now point to Manchester.

BARNES: Here, sir.

TEACHER: Wrong again! Barnes, you haven't listened. Now try again. Point to Southampton.

BARNES: Here, sir.

TEACHER: That's right at last. Sit down—and in future, listen! Now boys, I'll give you an exercise. Put this map into your notebooks. Then write the names of these towns on your maps: London, Edinburgh, Cardiff, Liverpool, Glasgow, Manchester, Southampton.

A BOY: Please, sir, I haven't got a pencil.

TEACHER: Take one from my table here.

A BOY: Please, sir, I've filled my book.

TEACHER: Take one from the cupboard.

(*Barnes is talking to another boy*)

Barnes, don't talk. Have you finished your work?

BARNES: No, sir.

TEACHER: You've wasted enough time today. Get on with your work—and do it well or you won't go home at four o'clock.

Answer these questions:

1 What time do boys and girls start and finish school in your country?
2 What is homework?
3 What games do schoolboys play in your country?
4 Some boys in the picture on page 99 are looking out of the window. What are they looking at?
5 What is a map?
6 Is Glasgow in England, Scotland or Wales?
7 The teacher has given the boys an exercise. What was the exercise?
8 What did the boys in the classroom have on their desks?
9 It is five o'clock, and the classroom is empty. Where have all the boys gone?

New Words

the autumn ('ɔːtəm)
  a class (klɑːs)
  a classroom ('klɑːsruːm)
    cricket ('krikit)
  a cupboard ('kʌbəd)
 an exercise ('eksəsaiz)
  a field (fiːld)
    football ('futbɔːl)
  a game (geim)
    homework ('houmwəːk)
  a lesson ('lesn)
  a map (mæp)
  a note-book ('noutbuk)
the spring (spriŋ)
  a teacher ('tiːtʃə)
    trousers ('trauzəz)
the winter ('wintə)

  Barnes (bɑːnz)
  Cardiff ('kɑːdif)
  Edinburgh ('edinbrə)
  England ('iŋglənd)
  Glasgow ('glɑːzgou)
  Great Britain ('greit 'britn)
  Liverpool ('livəpuːl)
  Scotland ('skɔtlənd)
  Southampton ('sauθ'æmptən)
  Thompson ('tɔmsn)
  Wales (weilz)

to fill (fil)
  filled (fild)
to finish ('finiʃ)
  finished ('finiʃt)
to listen ('lisn)
  listened ('lisnd)
to play (plei)
  played (pleid)
to point (pɔint)
  pointed ('pɔintid)
to remember (ri'membə)
  remembered (ri'membəd)
to try (trai)
  tried (traid)
to waste (weist)
  wasted ('weistid)

mine (main)
his[2] (hiz)
hers (həːz)
ours (auəz)
yours (jɔːz)
theirs (ðɛəz)

another (ə'nʌðə)
enough (i'nʌf)
usually ('juːʒuəli)

Sentence Patterns

35 Present Perfect tense

(a) *Regular verbs*

Susan has (Susan's) typed all the letters.
He has (He's) remembered all the names.

The boys have worked all the morning.
They have (They've) listened to the lesson.

I have (I've) filled my book.
We have (We've) started the first exercise.
You have (You've) wasted enough time today.

(b)   Irregular verbs—Participle same as Past tense

Tom has (Tom's) sold his old car.
She has (She's) put the map into the cupboard.

They have (They've) read all the books in this cupboard.
I have (I've) found your watch in the garden.
We have (We've) brought some wine and some beer.
You have (You've) got all these answers right.

(c)   Irregular verbs—Participle different from Past tense

The teacher has taken the map from the wall.
She has (She's) drunk two cups of coffee.
He has (He's) done his homework.
This bag has fallen out of your car.

They have (They've) gone home.
I have (I've) forgotten your name.
You have (You've) broken that window.

36 Present Perfect tense—Negative

(a)   Regular verbs

Barnes has not (hasn't) answered all the questions.
Susan has not (hasn't) telephoned her boy-friend today.

You have not (haven't) worked hard this morning.
We have not (haven't) played football this winter.
I have not (haven't) cooked breakfast.

(b)   Irregular verbs—Participle same as Past tense

He has not (hasn't) said a word all the evening.
She has not (hasn't) made a cake for us.

You have not (haven't) put your books away.
They have not (haven't) brought their friends with them.
I have not (haven't) read those letters.

(c)   Irregular verbs—Participle different from Past tense

She has not (hasn't) worn her new coat.

He has not (hasn't) eaten all his breakfast.

We have not (haven't) seen him today.
You have not (haven't) drunk your wine.
They have not (haven't) gone to bed.

37 Present Perfect tense—Questions

(a) *Regular verbs*

Has she remembered all the shopping?
Has he finished his work?

Have you enjoyed the evening?
Have they started the game?

(b) *Irregular verbs—Participle same as Past tense*

Has she bought a new coat?
Has he left school?

Have you had a nice evening?
Have I brought the wrong book?
Have they met Mr Robinson?

(c) *Irregular verbs—Participle different from Past tense*

Has she spoken to you about this?
Has he come back?

Have I rung the wrong bell?
Have we taken your books?

Exercises

A. Put the verbs in these sentences into the Present Perfect tense.

(a) Susan is finishing work
for the day. She is
putting her typewriter
away in a cupboard. She
is putting on her coat.
She is saying good-bye
to Mr Robinson. She is
leaving the office.

(b) Tom is driving his car from the factory. He is waiting for Susan at the corner of the street. He is bringing her some flowers. He is taking her home. He is having tea with the Brown family.

B. Put these words into the right places in this conversation:

my, his, her, your, our, their, hers, mine, ours

TEACHER: Barnes, where's *your* pen?

BARNES: I gave it to ... sister yesterday, sir. She left ... in a shop last week.

TEACHER: Where's ... pen now?

BARNES: ... sister gave it to ... boy-friend.

TEACHER: Where was ... pen?

BARNES: He left ... pen in a shop last week, too.

TEACHER: Do you always leave ... pens in shops?

BARNES: No, sir. We sometimes leave ... pens in trains. Last week, ... father left ... in a bank.

TEACHER: Well, take ... And bring it back to ... table at the end of the lesson.

C. The Thompsons

Make negative sentences with these words:

Example: the Thompsons, run, across, street

The Thompsons don't run across the street.

1   the Thompsons, eat, marmalade, knife

2   Tommy Thompson, write, walls

3   Mrs Thompson, smoke, cigarettes

4 Joan Thompson, play, street

5 Mr Thompson, shout, children

6 Tommy Thompson, hit, dog

7 Joan Thompson, leave, coat, floor

8 Tommy Thompson, break, windows

9 the Thompsons, put, feet, table

10 Mr Thompson, drive, fast, town

the floor (flɔː)   to smoke (smouk)

D. *Put the right form of the verb in brackets into these sentences:*

Fred is nine years old. He (*go*) to school every day. He (*live*) near the school, so he (*walk*) to school each morning. Today he (*be*) late. He (*run*) to school. He (*run*) across the street. A car (*come*) down the street. The car (*go*) very fast. '(*Stop*), Fred! Don't (*run*) across the street!'
Oh, dear! It (*be*) too late. The car (*hit*) Fred. The driver (*get*) out of his

car and (*stand*) near Fred. An ambulance (*come*) and the men (*put*) Fred
into the ambulance.
an ambulance ('æmbjuːləns)

E. Write eight sentences about your classroom.

Who is he?

A man is looking at a picture on the wall. He says to his friends:
'I haven't any sisters or brothers, but that man's father is my father's
son.
Who is the man in the picture?'

Unit 13

Tom and Susan Go Dancing

It is Saturday afternoon. Susan and her boy-friend Tom are in London; they came by car this morning. After lunch Susan wanted to do some shopping in Oxford Street and Tom wanted to go to the Motor Show. So they arranged to meet for a meal at six o'clock.

Every year there is a Motor Show at Earls Court, a big hall in London. All the car makers have stands and bring their new cars; they hope to sell a lot of these new cars to the people at the Show. Tom Smith always enjoys the Motor Show. He likes to look at the new cars and talk about them to the men on the stands. He bought a new car last year, so this year he will only look.

Susan likes to walk round the big stores in Oxford Street. Today she has bought a hat, some gloves, a handbag and some shoes. She has been in and out of dozens of shops, and now she is tired and ready for a meal. She arranged to meet Tom at a restaurant in Soho. It is now six o'clock, and there he is, waiting for her outside.

Now they have finished their meal and Tom is going to pay the bill.
They have had fruit juice, steaks, a sweet and then coffee. Tom has
drunk beer with his meal and Susan has drunk lager.

It is half past ten, and Susan and Tom are at a discotheque. There are
a lot of young people dancing in a small room. The room is dark,
except for some coloured lights—red, blue, green and orange. It is
very hot and the music is loud. A 'disc-jockey' is putting records on
the record-player, and telling the dancers about the records.

At midnight Susan and Tom decided to drive home. But half-way to

Bishopton their car stopped. They had enough petrol and the tyres were all right. Tom decided to go to a garage to get help. They walked two miles and found a garage. The man from the garage came back with them and mended the car. They got home at three o'clock in the morning. Mrs Brown was very worried. She doesn't like Susan to be out very late at night.

TOM: Hello, Susan. Have you had a good afternoon?
SUSAN: Yes, but I've walked in and out of shops, and now I'm tired. And I'm hungry.
TOM: I am too. What shall we have? Steaks?
SUSAN: Yes. Fruit juice first, then steak. I like mine well done. And after that a nice sweet.
TOM: What will you have to drink?
SUSAN: Lager, please.
TOM: And I'll have beer. Waiter!

              *   *   *

TOM: What have you bought today?
SUSAN: I wanted to buy a new coat, but I didn't see a nice one. I've bought some gloves, a handbag and some shoes. I saw a nice trouser suit, but it was a lot of money so I decided not to get it. Did you enjoy the Motor Show?
TOM: Yes. I've seen every new car in the Show. There are some very good new cars this year.
SUSAN: Do you want to buy another new car?
TOM: No. I bought the Jaguar only last year. Where

shall we go this evening? Shall we go to a cinema?

SUSAN: I want to go dancing. Shall we go to a discotheque?

TOM: All right. There's a good one near here. There are always a lot of people on Saturday night— and I like the disc-jockey there.

Thank you, waiter. The beer's mine, and the lager's yours, Susan.

(*In the car, half-way to Bishopton*)

SUSAN: We've stopped. What's happened?

TOM: There's something wrong with the car.

SUSAN: Have you enough petrol?

TOM: Yes. I'll get out and see what's wrong.

(*He gets out to look*)

SUSAN: What's wrong?

TOM: I don't know. I haven't found it.

SUSAN: Have you looked at the tyres?

TOM: Yes, they're all right. There's a garage near here.

SUSAN: It's very late—and I'm tired.

TOM: Come with me. I don't want to leave you here; it's very dark.

SUSAN: All right. Have you locked the car?

TOM: Yes. We shall be home very late. What will your mother say?

SUSAN: Oh, don't worry about her now. Come on!

(*At the Browns' house*)

MRS BROWN: Where have you two been? It's very late.

SUSAN: We've been to a discotheque in London. We've been dancing.

MRS BROWN: Until this time? It's three o'clock in the morning. I don't like you to be out so late, Susan.

TOM: I'm sorry, Mrs Brown. Something went wrong with the car. We walked to a garage: it was two miles. Then the man from the garage mended the car.

Answer these questions:

1 Where has Tom been today?
2 What is a Motor Show?
3 Where has Susan been today?
4 Why didn't she buy the trouser suit?
5 Has Tom bought a car today?
6 When did he buy his new car?
7 Where did Tom and Susan have their meal?
8 Why did they stop half-way back to Bishopton?
9 Who mended their car?
10 What time did they get home?

New Words

a bill (bil)
a cinema ('sinəmə)
a 'disc jockey' ('disk 'dʒɔki)
a discotheque ('diskoutek)
a hall (hɔːl)
a handbag ('hænd'bæg)
  help (help)
  juice (dʒuːs)
  lager ('laːgə)
a meal (miːl)
  music ('mjuːzik)
  petrol ('petrəl)
a restaurant ('restərɔŋ)
  something ('sʌmθiŋ)
a stand (stænd)
a store (stɔː)
a sweet (swiːt)
a trouser suit ('trauzə 'sjuːt)
a tyre ('taiə)
a waiter ('weitə)

Earls Court ('əːlz 'kɔːt)
Motor Show ('moutə 'ʃou)

Oxford Street ('ɔksfəd 'striːt)
Soho ('souhou)

to arrange, arranged (ə'reindʒ, ə'reindʒd)
to decide, decided (di'said, di'saidid)
to happen, happened ('hæpən, 'hæpənd)
to hope, hoped (houp, houpt)
to lock, locked (lɔk, lɔkt)
to mend, mended (mend, 'mendid)
to pay, paid (pei, peid)

coloured ('kʌləd)
expensive (ik'spensiv)
green (griːn)
half-way ('haːf 'wei)
loud (laud)
orange ('ɔrindʒ)
tired ('taiəd)
worried ('wʌrid)

except (ik'sept)

Sentence Patterns

38 Verb and Infinitive

Susan wanted to do some shopping.
He likes to look at the new cars.
They hope to sell a lot of new cars.

They arranged to meet at a restaurant.
They decided to drive home.

She doesn't like to be out late at night.
Tom doesn't want to go shopping.

She decided not to buy the blue coat.

Do you want to buy a new car?
Does Tom like to go to the Motor Show?
Did we arrange to meet at six o'clock?
Did you decide to go dancing?

39 Possessive Pronouns

This is my hat.	This hat is mine.
This is your pencil.	This pencil is yours.
That is his coat.	That coat is his.
Those are her books.	Those books are hers.
These are their note-books.	These note-books are theirs.
These are our cars.	These cars are ours.
Is that his coat?	Is that coat his?
Are these your letters?	Are these letters yours?
Are these our tickets?	Are these tickets ours?
Are these their pencils?	Are these pencils theirs?

Exercises

A. Put the verbs in brackets into the Present Perfect tense.

The Browns are watching television. Susan has gone into the kitchen to make tea. David is telling her about the play on television.

SUSAN (*from the kitchen*): What (*happen*), David?

DAVID: A car (*stop*) outside the bank. Two men (*get*) out. One man is sitting in the car. The two men (*take*) a bag from the car. They (*go*) into the bank.

SUSAN (*still in the kitchen*): Yes. Now what (*happen*)?

DAVID: A police car (*stop*) at each end of the street. Now a man (*open*) a window in the bank. He (*wave*) to the police cars. They (*drive*) up on each side of the thieves' car. Two policemen (*get*) out of each police car. Now the thieves (*come*) out of the bank. They (*get*) the bag in their hands. Now they (*see*) the policemen. They (*start*) to run.

SUSAN (*coming into the sitting-room*): All right. I (*finish*) the tea. Now I'm going to watch the play.

a kitchen ('kitʃn)   a play (plei)
   television ('telivizn)   to watch (wɔtʃ)

B. Fred hasn't been a good boy at school today.

(a) What hasn't he done?

Example: wash, face   *He hasn't washed his face.*

1 eat, breakfast
2 bring, books, school
3 do, homework
4 listen, teacher
5 give, right answers
6 answer, teacher's questions
7 write, name, exercise book
8 remember, lesson
9 finish, exercise
10 work, hard, school

(b) Now ask Fred questions with the words in (a)

Example: wash, face   *Have you washed your face?*

hard (haːd)   to wash (wɔʃ)

C. Finish these sentences, using a *to*-infinitive:
1 Mr Brown told David ...
2 Mrs Brown asked Susan ...
3 David wants ...
4 Susan likes ...
5 Tom hopes ...
6 Tom and Susan arranged ...
7 Mr and Mrs Brown have decided ...
8 You'll have ...
9 Susan and her friends are going ...
10 David doesn't want ...

D. Example: When will Susan and Tom go to London? (tomorrow)

They'll go to London tomorrow.

1 When will they get to London?   (at half past nine)
2 When will they meet for tea?   (at five o'clock)
3 When will Tom buy a new car?   (next week)
4 What colour will the car be?   (red and black)
5 When will they get home?   (at three o'clock in the morning)
6 Where will Susan buy her handbag?   (in Oxford Street)
7 How long will they be in the restaurant?   (for about an hour)
8 Where will they go then?   (to a discotheque)
9 Who will mend their car?   (a man from a garage)

Unit *13*

E. *Make questions from these sentences:*

1 Susan is buying a handbag.
2 She has bought a hat.
3 She is going to buy a tie for her father.
4 She came to London by train.
5 They got to London at half past nine.
6 Susan likes to go shopping.
7 She will meet Tom at Piccadilly Circus.
8 They will have a meal together.
9 Tom wanted to buy a new car.
10 He has seen a nice one at the Motor
Show.

together (tə'geðə)

Office workers

A young man started work in a large government office. At the end of his first day, he came home and his father asked him some questions.
'And how many people work in your office?' he began.
'Oh, about half the people there!' his son answered.

government ('gʌvənmənt)

Unit 14

Sunday Morning

It is Sunday morning. Mr Brown is in his garden. Mr and Mrs Brown sometimes go to church on Sunday morning, but today it is a fine day so Mr Brown is working hard in his garden. You can see him in this picture; he is digging happily with a garden fork and a spade. Mr Brown can grow very good vegetables and flowers. Each week he cuts the grass and keeps the garden tidy. It is sometimes cold and wet and he can't work in the garden, but today it is fine and warm.

Mrs Brown is working busily in her kitchen. She is cooking lunch for the family. It is hot in the kitchen, so the door is open. Mrs Brown enjoys cooking, and she can cook well. She cooks by gas, but she has an electric iron, an electric washing-machine and an electric kettle. Mr Brown has brought some vegetables from the garden. Mrs Brown has put the meat in the oven, and she can now wash the vegetables and put them in saucepans. Lunch will be ready at a quarter to one.

David is still in bed. He was out very late last night. He plays a guitar in a pop-group. David has long hair, and in the evenings he wears blue jeans. His father and mother don't like this, but David works well at school all the week, and on Saturday and Sunday he likes to be different. This afternoon he will go out on his motor-cycle with some friends. They will ride fast along the roads and make a lot of noise.

Susan and Tom are at church. The church service will finish at about twenty past twelve. Lunch will be ready at a quarter to one, so they will come home quickly. This afternoon they will go to the sea in Tom's car. It isn't cold today, so they can swim; Tom and Susan can swim well. After that they will have tea. They often go to the sea in summer.

MR BROWN (*at the kitchen door*): What vegetables do you want for lunch today, Mary?

MRS BROWN: Some potatoes and a nice cabbage, please.

MR BROWN: Have you any flowers in the house?

MRS BROWN: No. Please bring me some.

MR BROWN: Where's David?

MRS BROWN: He's still in bed.

MR BROWN: Lazy boy! Why can't he come and help me in the garden?

MRS BROWN: He was out very late last night.

MR BROWN: Yes, I know. He was wasting his time dancing and playing that guitar.

MRS BROWN: He works very hard at school all the week, John.

MR BROWN: Yes, but why doesn't he cut his hair? He always looks so untidy. And the clothes he wears!

MRS BROWN: All the boys of his age wear clothes like that. They have to wear tidy clothes at school, so in the evenings and at the week-end they like to wear something different.

MR BROWN: Then he'll go out on that motor-cycle this afternoon and ride noisily with his friends through the town and along the roads. Old people will be asleep quietly on Sunday afternoon and these noisy boys will wake them up. Oh, dear!

MRS BROWN: Yes, John. Now please bring the vegetables; I want to cook them.

SUSAN (*coming into the kitchen*): Hello, Mother! Is lunch ready?

MRS BROWN: Yes. I'll put it on the table now. Who was at church this morning?

SUSAN: Mrs Morton, the Jones family—oh, and old Mr Campbell. Where's Father?

MRS BROWN: In the garden. He's cutting the grass. Tell him to come in now, Tom, or his lunch will be cold. You can carry the dishes into the dining-room, Susan.

MR BROWN (*coming in from the garden*): Hello, you two. Lunch ready? Good! I'll wash, and then we'll have it.

MRS BROWN: John! Look at the dirt on your shoes. Please take them off. Don't bring dirt from the garden into my kitchen. I want to keep it clean.

MR BROWN: I'm sorry, my dear. I'll leave these shoes in the garage.

MRS BROWN: Hurry up, dear. Lunch is ready.

Answer these questions:

1 When can't Mr Brown work in his garden?
2 What does he do in his garden each week?
3 What time will lunch be ready?
4 Why will Tom and Susan come home quickly from church?
5 What will Mr Brown do before lunch?
6 What will David do on Sunday afternoon?
7 What does David do on Saturday evenings?
8 What does Mr Brown want David to do this morning?
9 David plays in a 'pop-group'. What does he play?
10 What clothes do David and his friends wear at school?

New Words

a church (tʃɜːtʃ)	an iron ('aiən)
dirt (dɜːt)	jeans (dʒiːnz)
a dish (diʃ)	a kettle ('ketl)
a family ('fæmili)	meat (miːt)
gas (gæs)	noise (nɔiz)
a guitar (gi'tɑː)	an oven ('ʌvn)

a pop-group ('popgru:p)

a saucepan ('sɔ:spən)

a service ('sərvis)

a spade (speid)

a washing-machine
 ('wɔʃiŋmə'ʃi:n)

a week-end ('wi:kend)

Campbell ('kæmbəl)

can, can't, could (kæn, ka:nt,
 kud)

to cut, cut (kʌt, kʌt)

to dig, dug (dig, dʌg)

to grow, grew, grown (grou, gru:,
 groun)

to help, helped (help, helpt)

to keep, kept (ki:p, kept)

to ride, rode, ridden (raid, roud,
 'ridn)

to swim, swam, swum (swim,
 swæm, swʌm)

to wake, woke, woken (weik,
 wouk, 'woukn)

along (ə'lɔŋ)

asleep (ə'sli:p)

busily ('bizili)

different ('difrənt)

electric (i'lektrik)

fine (fain)

happily ('hæpili)

lazy ('leizi)

like (laik)

long (lɔŋ)

noisily ('nɔizili)

open ('oupən)

quick (kwik)

quickly ('kwikli)

quietly ('kwaiətli)

still (stil)

tidy ('taidi)

untidy (ʌn'taidi)

40 'Can'

(a) Mr Brown can grow good vegetables.
Mrs Brown can cook nice meals.
Susan and Tom can swim well.

You can see Mr Brown in this picture.
It is warm, so they can swim today.
You can have your lunch now.

(b) David can't swim very well.
Tom can't play a guitar.
Susan can't cook as well as her mother.

He can't work in the garden on wet days.
It is cold, so the children can't swim today.
You can't have a holiday this afternoon.

(c) Can Susan drive a car?
Can these people speak English?
Can David play a guitar?

Can I come in?
Can you go dancing with me this evening?
What can I have for lunch?
Where can I buy a packet of cigarettes?

41 Adverbs

Mr Brown is digging happily in his garden.
Mrs Brown is working busily in the kitchen.
They came home quickly.
The boys rode noisily through the town.

David works hard at school.
Mrs Brown can cook well.
David was out late last night.
They drove fast through the town.

The Browns sometimes go to church on Sunday.
These boys always look so untidy.
They often go to the sea on Sunday.

42 Time—minutes

		Railway Time-tables
What's the time, please?		
It's five minutes past two.	2.5 A.M. or	02.05 or
It's five past two.	2.5 P.M.	14.05
It's two five.		
It's ten minutes past two.	2.10 A.M. or	02.10 or
It's ten past two.	2.10 P.M.	14.10
It's two ten.		
It's twenty minutes past two.	2.20 A.M. or	02.20 or
It's twenty past two.	2.20 P.M.	14.20
It's two twenty.		

It's twenty-five minutes past two. 2.25 A.M. or 02.25 or
It's twenty-five past two.   2.25 P.M.   14.25
It's two twenty-five.

It's twenty-five minutes to three. 2.35 A.M. or 02.35 or
It's twenty-five to three.   2.35 P.M.   14.35
It's two thirty-five.

It's twenty minutes to three. 2.40 A.M. or 02.40 or
It's twenty to three.   2.40 P.M.   14.40
It's two forty.

It's ten minutes to three. 2.50 A.M. or 02.50 or
It's ten to three.   2.50 P.M.   14.50
It's two fifty.

It's five minutes to three. 2.55 A.M. or 02.55 or
It's five to three.   2.55 P.M.   14.55
It's two fifty-five.

43 Impersonal 'it'—weather

(a)

It	is 's is not isn't	raining cold fine wet	today.
	was was not wasn't	warm a fine day	yesterday.

(b)

Is	it	raining cold fine	today?
Was		wet warm a fine day	yesterday?

Exercises

A. Put one of these adverbs into the right place in each of these sentences:
happily, busily, quickly, noisily, quietly, hard, well, late, fast, sometimes,
always, often

1 The Browns go to the theatre on Saturday.
2 It was late, so she ate her breakfast.
3 People usually speak in church.
4 The children are playing in the sea.
5 The manager comes to the office at nine o'clock.
6 Susan is working at her desk.
7 David came home last night.
8 It isn't raining in England.
9 Don't drive through the town, Tom.
10 Mr Brown walks to the station in the morning.
11 Mrs Brown can cook.
12 'Work at school, David.'

B. Put can *or* can't *into these sentences:*

1 Mrs Brown ... cook a hot dinner in five minutes.
2 Mr Brown ... cut the grass in half an hour.
3 You ... go from London to Glasgow in an hour.
4 A man ... carry a bicycle but he ... carry a car.
5 Mrs Brown ... play football.
6 A boy of eighteen ... drive a car in England.
7 Susan ... type well.
8 A dog ... speak, but it ... run.
9 A small boy ... run but he ... drive a car.
10 David ... play a guitar but he ... drive a train.

C. Choose the right forms to make correct negative sentences:

1 The Browns (*isn't going, won't go, didn't go*) to church yesterday.
2 Mrs Brown (*isn't, won't, can't*) cutting the grass in the garden.
3 Susan (*isn't, doesn't, won't*) go shopping tomorrow.
4 David (*is, doesn't, was,*) play football every Saturday.
5 There (*aren't, were, are*) any cakes in this shop.
6 We (*haven't, won't, have*) any trees in our garden.
7 Bakers (*didn't, don't*) sell cabbages.
8 Mrs Brown (*isn't, doesn't,*) cook Sunday lunch every day.
9 Mr Brown (*isn't, won't, didn't*) eating oranges for his lunch.

D. Put the right word into these sentences:

1 I gave the flowers to (*her, she*).
2 We took the books from (*they, them*).
3 This is my friend; I met (*she, her*) at the station.
4 Mr Robinson took Susan and (*I, me*) to the theatre.
5 My father and (*me, I*) saw (*he, him*) in London yesterday.
6 They took (*us, we*) to their house for tea.
7 We sat behind (*they, them*) in the theatre.
8 Tom met Susan and went with (*her, she*) to the sea.
9 Susan said, 'My boy-friend often writes to (*I, me*).'
10 Mr Robinson's secretary gave (*him, he*) a cup of coffee.

E. Tell this story.

Still not perfect
A small schoolboy often wrote, 'I have went', instead of, 'I have gone'.
At last his teacher said: 'Stay after school this afternoon and write
I have gone a hundred times. Then you will remember it.'
When the teacher came back he found a letter from the boy on his desk.
It said:

   Dear Sir,
     I have wrote 'I have gone' a hundred times, and now I have went.
                                      Jim Stone.

instead (in'sted)
to stay (stei)

Unit 15

On the Farm

Susan woke up early on Monday morning. She looked out of her bedroom window; the sun was already shining brightly. Then she remembered it was a holiday at her factory and she didn't have to go to work. 'I'll drive down to Strawberry Farm and see Uncle Joe and Aunt Ethel,' she thought. 'Tom will lend me his car.'

At half past nine she was driving quietly along the country road which goes to Strawberry Farm. Birds were singing in the sky and a dog was barking on the other side of a field. Suddenly Susan came round

a corner in the road and nearly ran into a cow which was crossing the road. She stopped the car and waited for the cow to cross. It did not hurry! Then she drove on, but more slowly this time. She didn't want to hurry.

She left the car near the farm gate and soon she was walking through the farmyard to the house. In a corner of the farmyard she saw her

Uncle Joe. He was looking at some pigs which he was going to take to the market next day. Joe Stansbury is a big man with wide shoulders and a red face. He likes Susan and was very pleased to see her.

JOE STANSBURY: Hello, Susan. How nice to see you.

SUSAN: Isn't it a lovely day? I've got a holiday. So I've come to see you.

JOE STANSBURY: Very nice too. Your aunt *will* be pleased.

SUSAN: I've just seen one of your cows on the road, Uncle. I was driving along and I nearly ran into it.

JOE STANSBURY: Someone left the gate open. That's the fourth time this week. (*To one of his men*) George!

GEORGE: Yes, Mr Stansbury.

JOE STANSBURY: I want to see the man who left the gate open. Miss Susan's just seen one of our cows in the road. She nearly ran into it. Get it in, will you?

GEORGE: All right, Mr Stansbury. I'll see to it.

JOE STANSBURY: Are you ready for a cup of tea, Susan? Your aunt's in the kitchen. I want to get these pigs into the van. I'm going to take them to the market. I've just given them their food.

Susan found her Aunt Ethel in the farmhouse kitchen. It was a big, cool room with a stone floor. Her aunt was cooking busily. She was a pretty woman and she always managed to look smart.

ETHEL: Hello, Susan, what a nice surprise. I've just finished this cooking, so we'll stop for a cup of tea. Try some of these cakes—I've just made them.

SUSAN: They're lovely, Auntie. You're a very good cook.

ETHEL: A farmer's wife has to be a good cook, my dear. Farmers are men who are always hungry.

SUSAN: The farm's looking well at the moment. Are you busy?

ETHEL: We're always busy on a farm, from January until December.

SUSAN: The corn will soon be ready in this hot sunshine.

ETHEL: Next month, in July, we shall cut the grass for hay, and in August or early September we shall harvest the corn. We'll be very busy then.

SUSAN: Perhaps David will come for a week or two to help you. He's going to Switzerland for three weeks from the second of August to stay with some friends who were in England last year, but he can come before then.

ETHEL: We'll be pleased to see him. Will you have another cup of tea?

SUSAN: No, thanks. That was very nice.

ETHEL: Now we'll go to see the chickens. I was cooking for three hours this morning, so I didn't get the eggs. We'll go and get them now. Then you can have some of them to take home.

SUSAN: Thanks very much. How many chickens have you got now?

ETHEL: A hundred and fifty. You can have one for your Sunday dinner.

SUSAN: That's very kind. Now I'll help you get the eggs. Where shall we start?

ETHEL: In the chicken-houses; there'll be a lot of eggs there. Then we'll look under the trees. I often find eggs there. I'll take this basket, and here's one for you. We'll come back for the third one later.

Answer these questions:

1 Why did Susan decide to spend a day with her aunt and uncle?
2 What was Susan doing at half past nine?
3 Susan nearly ran into a cow. What was the cow doing?
4 What was Joe Stansbury doing in the farmyard?
5 What was Mrs Stansbury doing in the kitchen?
6 Where was Joe Stansbury going to take the pigs?
7 Who was David going to see in Switzerland?
8 Why didn't Ethel Stansbury get the eggs during the morning?
9 In which months do farmers (*a*) make hay, and (*b*) harvest corn?
10 Susan has just come home from the farm. What did she bring with her?

New Words

an au nt (ɑːnt)
  auntie ('ɑːnti)
a basket ('bɑːskit)
a bedroom ('bedruːm)
a chicken ('tʃikin)
corn (kɔːn)
the country ('kʌntri)
a cow (kau)
a farm (fɑːm)
a farmer ('fɑːmə)
a farmhouse ('fɑːmhaus)
a farmyard ('fɑːmjɑːd)

food (fuːd)
hay (hei)
a market ('mɑːkit)
a pig (pig)
a road (roud)
a shoulder ('ʃouldə)
a side (said)
a stone (stoun)
the sun (sʌn)
a surprise (sə'praiz)
an uncle ('ʌŋkl)

Ethel ('eθəl)
George (dʒɔːdʒ)
Joe Stansbury ('dʒou
    'stænzbri)
Strawberry ('strɔːbri)
Switzerland ('switzələnd)

January ('dʒænuəri)
February ('februəri)
March (maːtʃ)
April ('eipril)
May (mei)
June (dʒuːn)
July (dʒu'lai)
August ('ɔːgəst)
September (sep'tembə)
October (ɔk'toubə)
November (nou'vembə)
December (di'sembə)

to bark, barked (baːk, baːkt)
to cross, crossed (krɔs, krɔst)
to harvest, harvested ('haːvist,
    'haːvistid)
to lend, lent (lend, lent)
to manage, managed ('mæniʒ,
    'mænidʒd)

to shine, shone (ʃain, ʃɔn)
to sing, sang, sung (siŋ, sæŋ, sʌŋ)
to spend, spent (spend, spent)
to think, thought (θiŋk, θɔːt)

already (ɔːl'redi)
brightly ('braitli)
cool (kuːl)
just (dʒʌst)
later ('leitə)
lovely ('lʌvli)
nearly ('niəli)
slowly ('slouli)
someone ('sʌmwʌn)
suddenly ('sʌdnli)
which (witʃ)
who[2] (huː)

1st first (fəːst)
2nd second ('sekənd)
3rd third (θəːd)
4th fourth (fɔːθ)
5th fifth (fifθ)
6th sixth (siksθ)
12th twelfth (twelθ)
20th twentieth ('twentiəθ)
21st twenty-first ('twenti'fəːst)

Sentence Patterns

44 Past Continuous tense

Birds were singing in the sky.
Men were working in the fields.
We were looking for some eggs.
I was driving along the road.
Her aunt was cooking in the kitchen.
Susan was walking across the farmyard.

45 Relative Clauses—'who', 'which', 'that'

(a) For people—'who'

I'm going to take the pigs to the man who bought them.
Farmers are men who are always hungry.
It was George who left the gate open.
Mrs Brown has a sister who lives in the country.

(b) For things—'which', 'that'

This is the road which (that) goes to Strawberry Farm.
She nearly ran into a cow which (that) was crossing the road.
Was it your dog which (that) was barking all night?
Ours is the farmhouse which (that) has a red gate.

46 'Have just'

I have (I've) just seen one of your cows in the road.
We have (We've) just had lunch.
Susan has just driven to the farm.
The farmer has just sold some pigs.
I have (I've) just made these cakes.

Exercises

A. Make sentences from these words with the same form of the verb as in the example:

Example: sun, shine, sky

The sun was shining in the sky.

1 Susan, drive, road
2 she, go, visit, aunt
3 cow, cross, road
4 farmer, stand, farmyard
5 he, look, pigs
6 Aunt Ethel, make, tea
7 they, talk, kitchen
8 they, look, eggs, chicken-houses
9 David, stay, friends, Switzerland
10 Mrs Brown, shop, Bishopton

to talk (tɔːk)

B. *Finish these sentences.*

Use the right form of the verb in brackets:

1 Tom has just (*finish*) work.
2 He has just (*say*) good-night to the manager.
3 He has just (*leave*) the factory.
4 He has just (*get*) into his car.
5 He has just (*drive*) away in his car.

6 Fred has just (*throw*) a stone through a window.
7 He has just (*break*) the window.
8 Fred's father has just (*come*) home.
9 He has just (*put*) his car in the garage.
10 Fred has just (*tell*) his father about the window.

to throw, threw, thrown (θrou, θruː, θroun)

C. Join these sentences, using *who* or *which*:

1 Susan went to see her aunt. She lives on a farm.
2 This is the dog. It was barking all night.
3 He met some friends. They were staying with the Browns.
4 This isn't the postman. He usually comes to our house.
5 He has a watch. It keeps very good time.

D. *Write the dates marked:*

Example: *Tuesday, 10th June*

June					July					August				
Sunday	①	8	15	22	29		6	13	20	27		3	10	17	24	31
Monday	2	9	16	23	30		7	14	21	28		4	11	18	25
Tuesday	3	⑩	17	24		1	8	15	22	29		⑤	12	19	26
Wednesday	4	11	18	25		2	9	16	23	30		6	13	20	27
Thursday	5	⑫	19	26		③	10	17	24	㉛		7	14	21	28
Friday	6	13	⑳	27		④	11	18	25		1	8	15	22	29
Saturday	7	14	21	28		5	12	19	26		②	9	⑯	23	30

E. Example: There is a *book* on that table. (*pen*)

There are some pens on that table.

1 There is a *spoon* on that table. (*cup*)
2 There is a *woman* in that room. (*man*)
3 There is a *fork* near my plate. (*knife*)
4 There is a *handbag* in that cupboard. (*watch*)
5 There is an *orange* in this basket. (*cherry*)
6 There is a *cabbage* in this shop. (*potato*)
7 There is a *piece of cake* on the table. (*loaf of bread*)
8 She is eating a *chocolate*. (*sandwich*)
9 He has drunk a *cup of tea*. (*glass of wine*)
10 He has a *packet of cigarettes* in his pocket. (*box of matches*)
11 She has a *glove* on her *hand*. (*shoe, foot*)

a cherry ('tʃeri)   a piece (piːs)
  cherries   a sandwich ('sænwidʒ)
a chocolate ('tʃɔkələt)

The farmer comes to town

A farmer and his wife from the country were in London for the first time. They saw in the window of a restaurant:

'LUNCHES 12 until 2—40p'

'Come on, Mary,' said the farmer, 'that's not expensive. We can sit there and eat for two hours for forty pence.'

Unit 16

A Visit to London

The Browns have some Swiss friends, Margrit and Edouard Erling. They are a brother and sister, the same ages as Susan and David. While they were in England last summer they stayed with the Browns in Bishopton. The Erlings didn't know London, so David and Susan took them to the West End and the City and showed them all the interesting places they wanted to see.

The City is small, but it is very important. Two thousand years ago the Romans built a town here. For hundreds of years people lived and worked here, but now nearly all the houses have gone. Instead, there are large offices. Thousands of people come here by train every morning, and when they have finished their work in the evening they go home again. At night the City is very quiet and empty.

In the West End there are theatres, cinemas, long streets of fine shops and many big houses. There are beautiful parks too. In the West End you will find most of the offices of the government.

David and Susan took their friends first to Buckingham Palace, the home of the Queen and the Royal Family. The Queen was coming out of the Palace in her car when they got there. Margrit and Edouard

were very pleased; they wanted to see the Queen while they were in England.

Then they walked down Whitehall, and saw the government offices. When they were crossing the road to Westminster Abbey, Big Ben, the clock on the Houses of Parliament, struck eleven. From Westminster they went down the River Thames by boat to the Tower of London;

there they saw the Queen's jewels. After they left the Tower they went into St Paul's Cathedral. Near St Paul's they saw the Mansion House, the home of the Lord Mayor of London. Each November there is a new Lord Mayor, and he lives in the Mansion House for a year.

After lunch, they got on a bus to the National Gallery. Here they saw many beautiful pictures.

They had dinner in a little restaurant in Soho, to which Susan and her boy-friend often go, and after dinner Susan and David took their

Swiss friends to a theatre. Margrit and Edouard know English well, so they enjoyed this. It was midnight when they got home after a very interesting day.

DAVID: This is Whitehall. All those big buildings are government offices. In November every year the Queen drives down Whitehall from Buckingham Palace when she goes to open Parliament. Many people come to watch her.

MARGRIT: What are those buildings at the end of the street?

DAVID: You know the building with the clock; that's the Houses of Parliament. The building near it with two towers is Westminster Abbey. Now we'll go by boat to the Tower. That's a place everyone visits while they are in London. It's near Tower Bridge.

EDOUARD: Is that the bridge they open to let boats go through?

DAVID: Yes. Now we're going under London Bridge. This bridge isn't old, but there was a bridge here many years ago which had houses and shops on it.

MARGRIT: Is that the Tower of London? But there are lots of towers there.

DAVID: Yes, but the one in the middle—the White Tower—is *the* Tower.

MARGRIT: How old is it?

DAVID: About a thousand years old. Years ago, kings and queens lived—and died—here.

SUSAN: I don't like the Tower. It's cold and grey, and it frightens me. Shall we go and have lunch now? I'm hungry.

DAVID: All right. There's an old restaurant near here you'll like. It's very good. And after we've had lunch we'll go back to the West End.

* * *

MARGRIT: Can we get to the National Gallery from here?

DAVID: Yes, we'll go by bus. Then you can see all the interesting buildings we pass on the way. That's the Bank of England. This is Fleet Street, with all the newspaper offices. Now we're in the Strand. Charing Cross Station is on the left, and now we are coming to Trafalgar Square. The National Gallery is on the right.

MARGRIT: How many pictures are there in the Gallery?

DAVID: I don't know. About two thousand, I think.

EDOUARD: Don't ask so many hard questions, Margrit. David can't tell you everything you want to know.

MARGRIT: All right. I'll ask an easy question. Where's the toilet?

SUSAN: Come on! I'll show you. Down these stairs.

Answer these questions:

1 When did the Erlings stay with the Browns?
2 When do the people who work in the City go home?
3 When did the Erlings see the Queen?
4 When did they hear Big Ben strike?
5 When did they visit St Paul's Cathedral?
6 How long does each Lord Mayor live in the Mansion House?
7 When does the Queen drive down Whitehall from Buckingham Palace?
8 What do you know about Tower Bridge?
9 What did they do after lunch?
10 What did David say about the Tower of London?

New Words

a boat (bout)
a bridge (bridʒ)
a building ('bildiŋ)
a city ('siti)
 everyone ('evriwʌn)
a jewel ('dʒuəl)
a king (kiŋ)
the middle ('midl)
 midnight ('midnait)
a park (paːk)
a place (pleis)
 queen (kwiːn)
a stair (stɛə)
a toilet ('tɔilit)
a visit ('vizit)

Big Ben ('big 'ben)
Buckingham Palace ('bʌkiŋəm 'pælis)
Charing Cross ('tʃæriŋ 'krɔs)
Fleet Street ('fliːt 'striːt)
the Lord Mayor ('lɔːd 'mɛə)
the Mansion House ('mænʃn 'haus)
the National Gallery ('næʃnəl 'gæləri)
the River Thames ('rivə 'temz)

the Romans ('roumənz)
St Paul's Cathedral (sənt 'pɔːlz kə'θiːdrəl)
Swiss (swis)
the Tower ('tauə)
Trafalgar Square (trə'fælgə 'skwɛə)
Westminster Abbey ('westminstə 'æbi)
Whitehall ('waithɔːl)

to build, built (bild, bilt)
to die, died (dai, daid)
to frighten, frightened ('fraitn, 'fraitnd)
to let, let (let, let)
to show, showed, shown (ʃou, ʃoud, ʃoun)
to strike, struck (straik, strʌk)

beautiful ('bjuːtiful)
easy ('iːzi)
grey (grei)
interesting ('intrəstiŋ)
left (left)
right[2] (rait)

royal ('rɔiəl)   ago (ə'gou)
same (seim)   really ('riəli)
thousand ('θauzənd)   when² (wen)
west (west)   while (wail)

Sentence Patterns

47 Time Clauses

'When'

They go home when they have finished their work.
It was midnight when they got home.
When they were crossing the road, the clock struck eleven.
When you've finished that you can have some more.

'While'

They stayed with the Browns while they were in England.
They wanted to see the Queen while they were in London.
While we were in the theatre someone took our car.
While you're waiting you can read this newspaper.

'Before'

They had lunch before they went to the National Gallery.
They're going to visit Oxford before they go back home.
Before you leave London, come and have dinner with us.

'After'

We'll go to the theatre after we've had dinner.
They're going to have dinner after they leave the theatre.
After they left the Tower they went to St Paul's.
After they have seen London they will visit Oxford.

'Until'

She stays at the office until she has finished her work.
'Don't got home until you have typed these letters, please.'
They watched until the Queen came out of the Palace.

48 Contact Clauses without Relatives

(a) For things

He showed them all the places they wanted to see.
This is the river we crossed in the train from Dover.
This is the bridge they open to let boats through.
I know a restaurant you'll like very much.

(b) For people

This is the man we met in Holland.
Is that the boy you saw at the station?
Susan wrote a letter to a girl she knows.
Mr Thompson is the man I wanted to meet.

Exercises

A. Finish these sentences:

1 ... until it was very late.
2 ... while she was waiting for a bus.
3 ... when you get home.
4 ... before it starts to rain.
5 ... after we have finished breakfast.
6 .. until the end of the summer.
7 ... while she was in London.
8 ... when I get my new car.
9 ... before we get too hungry.
10 ... after we left the theatre.

B. It is now seven o'clock in the evening.

Write ten sentences saying what each of these people was doing at eleven o'clock this morning.
Begin each sentence:

At eleven o'clock this morning ...

1 Mr Brown	2 Mrs Brown
3 Susan	4 David
5 Tom Smith	6 The policeman in Bishopton
7 Mr Jones, the greengrocer	8 Mr Stephens, the baker
9 you	10 your teacher

C. Put the right words into these sentences:

1 Yesterday David and Susan went ... their friends ... London.
2 They waited ... Buckingham Palace until the Queen came ...
3 They walked ... Whitehall ... Westminster Abbey.
4 Then they walked ... the road to the Houses of Parliament.
5 They went ... Westminster ... the Tower of London ... boat.
6 ... the Tower they saw the Queen's jewels.
7 They had lunch ... a restaurant ... the City.

8 Then they went ... bus ... the West End.
9 ... dinner they went ... a theatre.
10 They got home ... midnight.

D. Mr Roberts, the teacher, is talking to the boys in his class:

Don't close that window.

Write sentences like this, using these words:

1	open, door	7	play, school
2	drop, book	8	break, glass
3	put, map, on, wall	9	do, homework, class
4	take, pencils, cupboard	10	leave, room, end, lesson
5	drop, paper, floor	11	put, pencil, mouth
6	talk, during, lesson	12	bring, dog, school

to drop, dropped (drɔp, drɔpt)

E. Join these sentences together, leaving out the relatives *who* or *which*:
1 I can't find the pen. You lent it to me.
2 That's the man. We saw him at the theatre last night.
3 Can you remember the girl? You gave your book to her.
4 Have you seen the flowers? I brought them for your mother.
5 This is the car. Tom bought it at the Motor Show.

F. *Write ten or twelve sentences about a city or town you know well.*

The new baby

'Aunt Mary has a new baby,' a mother told her small daughter.
'What was wrong
with the old one?'
answered the little
girl.

baby ('beibi)

Unit 17

Camping Week-end

Last week-end Tom, Susan, David and David's new girl-friend, Helen, decided to go camping.

TOM: The papers say it's going to be the hottest week-end of the year. Shall we go camping?

SUSAN: Yes. We'll go to that place we went to last time. It's the nicest place we've been to, isn't it?

DAVID: All right! Helen and I'll go on my motor-bike and you two can take the tents in the car.

They set off on Friday evening and drove to their favourite camping place about thirty miles away. Here the fields slope south to a small stream, and a wood keeps out the wind from the north and east.

TOM: David and I'll put up the tents while you girls cook a meal.

DAVID: We'll need some eggs and milk from the farm,
shan't we?

SUSAN: No. We've brought enough with us for
tonight, haven't we, Tom?

TOM: Yes, but we'll need some more tomorrow.

In the night Susan woke up.

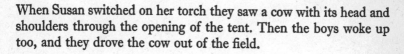

SUSAN: Helen, there's someone in the tent, isn't there?
Can you hear a noise?

HELEN: No, I can't. I'm asleep.

SUSAN: Ooh, something wet touched my face. Where's
my torch?

HELEN: It's under your pillow, isn't it?

When Susan switched on her torch they saw a cow with its head and
shoulders through the opening of the tent. Then the boys woke up
too, and they drove the cow out of the field.

TOM: We didn't shut the gate before we went to
sleep, did we?

SUSAN: Look at the mess. That cow's kicked over all
our things round the tent.

DAVID: And it's pulled up some of the tent ropes. We
shall have to put these back at once, shan't we?
The tents will blow away.

HELEN: Oh dear. And I'm still half asleep.

The next day was very hot. They went swimming in the stream and
lay in the grass sun-bathing. Tom and David brought milk and eggs
from the farm and the girls did the cooking. During the day it got
hotter and hotter—but that night, while they were asleep, it started
to rain. It rained and rained, until the water came into the tents.
When they woke up at three o'clock in the morning their bedclothes
were wet, the ground inside and outside the tents was wet—everyone
and everything was wet.

HELEN: I'm all wet.

SUSAN: So are we all, dear. And cold.

DAVID: We can't stay here like this, can we? We shall
have to go home.

TOM: All right. Put everything in the car.

HELEN: I can't find my coat. I'm getting wetter and
        wetter.
DAVID: Here's my torch. Now hurry, or you'll get
        wetter than ever.

They packed everything into Tom's car. But when they were ready
to go, David couldn't start his motor-bike. There was water in the
engine. So they all sat in the car getting colder and more miserable
until morning. It wasn't the happiest week-end of their lives.

Answer these questions:
 1 Who was Helen?
 2 How did they get to the camping-place?
 3 What did Susan say about their camping place?
 4 What did they do first when they got there?
 5 Where did they get their milk and eggs?
 6 Why did Susan wake up?
 7 What did Susan see when she switched on her torch?
 8 How did the cow get into the field?
 9 What happened when they woke up on the second night?
 10 David couldn't start his motor-bike. What was the matter with it?

New Words

bedclothes ('bedklouðz)
camping ('kæmpiŋ)
dear (diə)
an engine ('endʒin)
the ground (graund)
life (laif)
a mess (mes)
milk (milk)
an opening ('oupniŋ)
a pillow ('pilou)
a rope (roup)
a stream (striːm)
a tent (tent)
tonight (tə'nait)
a torch (tɔːtʃ)
water ('wɔːtə)
the wind (wind)
a wood (wud)
Helen ('helin)

to blow, blew, blown (blou, bluː, bloun)
to kick, kicked, (kik, kikt)

to lie, lay, lain (lai, lei, lein)
to need, needed (niːd, 'niːdid)
to pack, packed (pæk, pækt)
to pull, pulled (pul, puld)
to set off, set off ('set ɔf, 'set ɔf)
to shut, shut (ʃʌt, ʃʌt)
to slope, sloped (sloup, sloupt)
to sun-bathe, sun-bathed ('sʌnbeið, 'sʌnbeiðd)
to switch, switched (switʃ, switʃt)
to touch, touched (tʌtʃ, tʌtʃt)

east (iːst)
favourite ('feivrit)
miserable ('mizrəbl)
north (nɔːθ)
south (sauθ)

at once (ət'wʌns)
during ('djuːriŋ)
than (ðæn)

Sentence Patterns

49 Question-tags

(a) Expecting answer 'yes'

It's a nice place, isn't it?
There's someone in the tent, isn't there?
They're camping this week-end, aren't they?
We've brought enough milk, haven't we?
We'll need some eggs, shan't we?
She can swim well, can't she?

David still goes to school, doesn't he?
They live in Bishopton, don't they?
Tom bought a new car last week, didn't he?
They went camping last week, didn't they?

(b) *Expecting answer 'no'*

It isn't raining now, is it?
They're not enjoying this week-end, are they?
She hasn't brought any eggs, has she?
You won't drop that torch, will you?
She wasn't in London last week, was she?

Susan doesn't still go to school, does she?
You don't like the rain, do you, Helen?
They don't come here often, do they?
We didn't shut the gate, did we?

50 Comparison of Adjectives

'-er', '-est'

This is a nice place to camp in.
I know a nicer place than this for camping.
This is the nicest place we've been to.

The next day was very hot.
It was hotter in the afternoon than in the morning.
It's going to be the hottest week-end of the year.

Even in summer it is often cold at night.
Water in the sea is usually colder than water in the river.
It was the coldest night they could remember.

They live in a small house.
They bought a smaller house.
This is the smallest house I have ever seen.

'more', 'most'

They went to a beautiful place in the country.
Some places are more beautiful than others.
She is the most beautiful girl I have ever met.

David has an expensive motor-bike.
Tom will buy a more expensive car next year.
Helen always likes to buy the most expensive clothes.

It was a miserable night.
They were getting more miserable every minute.
This is the most miserable holiday I can remember.

There are some interesting old houses near here.
London is a more interesting city than Leeds or Manchester.
I will show you the most interesting places while you are in London.

Exercises

A. Write sentences with these question-tags at the end:

1 ..., isn't it?
2 ..., weren't they?
3 ..., hasn't she?
4 ..., don't they?
5 ..., didn't you?
6 ..., aren't I?
7 ..., can't they?
8 ..., isn't he?
9 ..., won't they?
10 ..., shan't we?

B. (a) Put in the right form of the adjective:

1 David is (*tall, taller, tallest*) than Susan.
2 It was a very (*hot, hotter, hottest*) day.
3 It is (*quiet, quieter, quietest*) in the country than in the town.
4 Tom drives a very (*fast, faster, fastest*) car.
5 Today is the (*cold, colder, coldest*) day we have had this year.

(b) Put in the right form of the adjective:

6 It was the (*miserable*) night of their lives.
7 Her shoes were (*expensive*) than her hat.
8 Leeds is an (*important*) city in the north of England.
9 I think Westminster Abbey is (*beautiful*) than St Paul's Cathedral.
10 This is the (*interesting*) book I have read for a long time.

C. (a) Write four sentences telling what Susan likes to do.

149

(*b*) Write four sentences telling what David *wants* to do.
(*c*) Write four sentences saying what Mr Brown *told* David to do.
(*d*) Write four sentences saying what Mrs Brown *asked* Susan to do.

D. *Put the verbs in brackets into the right form:*

George and Joan (*live*) in a small house in London. They (*stand*) in the sitting-room of their house. They (*just come*) back from a holiday in the country. They (*arrive*) at the house five minutes ago.

'What (*happen*)?' (*say*) Joan, as she (*look*) round at the untidy room. 'Someone (*be*) in the house. They (*take*) everything out of the cupboards and (*throw*) them on the floor. (*look*), George, they (*break*) all those glasses and (*pour*) wine on the carpet. I (*think*) I'm (*cry*).'

George is very angry. He (*pick*) up the telephone. 'I (*want*) the police,' he (*say*). 'Someone (*break*) into our house while we (*be*) away. I don't know what they (*take*). The place is very untidy.'

'(*look*)!' says Joan. 'They (*leave*) their gloves.'

'(*don't pick*) them up,' says George. '(*leave*) everything for the police. When the police (*go*) you can tidy up.'

to arrive (ə'raiv)
to cry, cried (krai, kraid)

a minute ('minit)
to pick up ('pik 'ʌp)
to tidy up ('taidi 'ʌp)

E. Put *some* or *any* into the blanks in these sentences:

1 There are ... fine churches in London.
2 Are there ... cars in this picture?
3 We usually see ... cars in a London street.
4 I can't see ... policemen in this picture.
5 ... people are going into the cathedral.
6 There are ... birds in the sky.
7 Are there ... birds on the ground?
8 ... people like visiting cathedrals.
9 Have you visited ... churches in England?
10 There aren't ... trees in this picture.

F. *Write ten or twelve sentences about a week-end or short holiday you enjoyed—*
   or did not enjoy.

Asking too much

Here is a story about an Irishman.
An Englishman was driving along a country road in Ireland and met a man carrying a large bag.
'Can I take you into town?' the Englishman asked.
The Irishman said, 'Thank you,' and got into the car.
In a few minutes the driver saw that the Irishman was sitting with the large bag still in his hand. 'Why don't you put your bag down?' he asked.
'Well,' answered the Irishman, 'you've given me a ride in your car. I can't ask you to carry my bag as well.'

Ireland ('aiǝlǝnd)
Irishman ('aiǝri ʃmǝn)

Unit 18

The Football Match

Last Saturday afternoon David Brown and his father went to a football match at the Bishopton football ground. There were fifteen thousand people there. They came from far and near because it was the most important match of the year at Bishopton. The Browns and many other Bishopton people think that theirs is the best team in the South of England.

At three o'clock the two teams came on the field. The Bishopton team (the 'home' team) were playing in blue and white shirts, the Easthampton City players (the visitors' team) were in red and white shirts.

The referee blew his whistle and the match began. For the first thirty minutes the Bishopton team were stronger and kept the ball in the Easthampton side of the field. Then, suddenly, an Easthampton player took the ball quickly up the field and scored the first goal. The crowd shouted loudly. Soon after this, the referee blew his whistle because it was 'half-time'.

In the second half of the match the Bishopton team were again the better players. They tried hard, and after ten minutes they scored their first goal. They scored again after a quarter of an hour; then, before the last whistle blew, they scored a third goal and so won the match. All the Bishopton people in the crowd were very pleased, and went home happily to tea.

MR BROWN: Well, that was a good game. The best we've seen this winter.

DAVID: Yes, I think so. Better than last week. Easthampton have a good team, but the Bishopton players won because they're faster.

MR BROWN: Come on, David. The crowd's moving. We'll catch that bus. Then we can meet your mother in town for tea.

DAVID: Is she coming into town this afternoon?

MR BROWN: Yes, she said so.

DAVID: Who are Bishopton playing next week?

MR BROWN: Cardiff City.

DAVID: Do you think they'll win?

MR BROWN: Yes, I think so. But Cardiff have a good team this year.

DAVID: Which team will win the Cup?

MR BROWN: Leeds have a good chance, but Manchester have a better.

DAVID: What about Chelsea?

MR BROWN: They have, perhaps, the best chance of all.

DAVID: Why do you think so?

MR BROWN: Because they have a very fast team and some of their players are very clever with the ball; they can think as well as run, and that's the most important thing in football.

DAVID: Here's our bus. I think we shall get on.

MR BROWN: I hope so. Good, we're the last ones on.

BUS CONDUCTOR: Fares please. Any more fares?

MR BROWN: Two into town, please.

BUS CONDUCTOR: Ten pence. Thank you.

DAVID: Can you get tickets for the Cup this year?

MR BROWN: Yes, I think so. Mr Brook knows the secretary of the Bishopton Football Club. He's said he'll get me two tickets.

DAVID: Can you get three? Tom wants to go.

MR BROWN: I hope so. But it's harder every year to get tickets because so many people want them. And they'll be more expensive this year. Here's our stop. We get off here. There's your mother, waiting to go for tea.

Answer these questions:

1 Why were there so many people at this match?
2 Why was the Bishopton team called the 'home' team?
3 Why did the crowd shout loudly?
4 Why did the Bishopton people go home happily?
5 Why did the Bishopton team win?
6 Why did David and his father hurry to catch the bus?
7 Why did David want three tickets for the 'Cup'?
8 Why did Mr Brown think Bolton will win the Cup?
9 What does 'tickets for the Cup' mean?
10 Why is it hard to get tickets for the Cup?

New Words

a ball (bɔːl)
a chance (tʃɑːns)
a club (klʌb)
a conductor (kənˈdʌktə)
a crowd (kraud)
a fare (fɛə)
a goal (goul)
  half-time (ˈhɑːf ˈtaim)
a match[2] (mætʃ)
a player (ˈpleiə)
a referee (refəˈriː)
  rugger (ˈrʌgə)
  Rugby Football (ˈrʌgbi ˈfutbɔːl)

soccer (ˈsɔkə)
Association Football
  (əˈsousieiʃn ˈfutbɔːl)
a stop (stɔp)
a team (tiːm)
a whistle (ˈwisl)
  Chelsea (ˈtʃelsi)
  Easthampton (ˈiːsthæmptən)

to catch, caught (kætʃ, kɔːt)
to move, moved (muːv, muːvd)
to score, scored (skɔː, skɔːd)
to win, won (win, wʌn)

better ('betə)	strong (strɔŋ)
best (best)	
clever ('klevə)	because (bi'kɔz)
far (fɑː)	so² (sou)
loudly ('laudli)	soon (suːn)

Sentence Patterns

51 Reason

(a) *'Why?' 'Because'*

Why did people come from far and near?
Because it was the most important match of the year.
Why did the referee blow his whistle?
Because it was half-time.
Why did the Bishopton team win?
Because they were faster.
Why is it hard to get tickets for the Cup?
Because so many people want them.

(b) *Reason clauses—'because'*

They came from far and near because it was an important match.
The referee blew his whistle because it was half-time.
The Bishopton players won because they were faster.
It's hard to get tickets because so many people want them.

52 *'I think so', 'I hope so'*

Do you think Bolton will win the Cup?	Yes, I think so.
Can you get three tickets for the Cup?	I hope so.
Is Mother coming into town today?	Yes, she said so.
Is it going to rain?	No, I don't think so.
Are Susan and Tom coming to the match?	They didn't say so.

Exercises

A. Finish these sentences, using *because:*

1 David wears untidy clothes at the week-end ...

2 Susan sometimes comes late to the office in the morning ...

3 It is difficult to get tickets for the Cup match ...

4 Susan decides to visit her aunt on the farm ...

5 The referee blew his whistle ...

Now give the first part of each of these sentences:

6 ... because it rained.

7 ... because they saw the Queen.

8 ... because the bus is full.

9 ... because he is not well.

difficult ('difiklt)   full (ful)

B. *Write sentences to which these could be the answers:*

1 I think so.
2 He said so.
3 No, I don't think so.
4 Yes, she hopes so.
5 He didn't say so.
6 We hope so.

C. Look at this picture, then put the right
verb from the list below into the
blanks in the passage.
Use the Present tense.

*call, finish, stop, fall,
give, bring, break, put,
blow, hurt*

One player ... on the ground. He ... his leg; perhaps he ... it. The referee
... his whistle, and the game ... They ... someone to help the hurt player.

This man ... a coat and ... this under the player's head. Now he ... him something to drink. When the player ... his drink, they will carry him off the field and the game will start again.

to call, called (kɔːl, kɔːld)   a leg (leg)

D. *Put the right possessive adjective or pronoun into the blanks in this passage:*

'It's raining, and I've left ... umbrella at home. Can I take ..., please?'
'No, I'm sorry, I want ... But John doesn't want ... He left ... umbrella in that cupboard. We all keep ... umbrellas there.'
'There's only one umbrella here. Is this John's or ...?'
'That's .... John must have ... umbrella with him.'
'It's raining hard. All the people have umbrellas.'
'All right. Take .... I shan't want it before six o'clock. I shall have ... tea before I go out.'

E. *Put the right form of the adjective into these sentences:*

1 Bishopton has one of (*good*) football teams in the South of England.
2 David is (*clever*) than Tom, but Tom is a (*good*) driver.
3 Susan usually likes (*expensive*) coat in the shop, but she doesn't always buy it.
4 This exercise is (*difficult*) than the last one.
5 David is sometimes (*tired*) of school; he thinks he will be (*happy*) when he leaves.
6 I can't stay here talking to you; I have (*important*) things to do.
7 We'll move our tents under those trees; the ground is (*dry*) there.
8 Susan is (*young*) than Tom, but (*old*) than David.
9 Mr Brown is a (*careful*) driver than David.
10 Some people think Paris is (*beautiful*) city they have ever seen.

F. *On Monday morning David told one of his friends at school about the football match on Saturday afternoon. Write what you think he said.*

The hole in the roof

Here is another story about an Irishman.
A friend found Paddy sitting in his house. There was a hole in the roof, and the rain came through on his head.
'Mend your roof, Paddy,' the friend said. 'The rain is coming through.'
'Do you want me to go up in this rain?' asked Paddy.
'No. Mend it on a fine day.'
'But the water doesn't come in then,' said Paddy.

roof (ruːf)
hole (houl)

Unit 19

Christmas Day

Christmas has come at last. In England the most important day is Christmas Day and not Christmas Eve. On Christmas Day people give presents to their family and friends and have their Christmas dinner.

The Browns' house is looking really beautiful. Yesterday Mr Brown and David were working all day putting up the holly and coloured paper over the doors and pictures. They put a big Christmas tree just inside the front door, and hung coloured electric lights along the branches. Everything looks very gay and exciting. Mrs Brown's cousins, Tom and Brenda Mason, with two small children, Jackie and Sheila, are staying with the Browns. Before bedtime on Christmas Eve the children called up the chimney to Father Christmas and told him what they wanted; then they hung up their stockings at the foot of their beds. 'If you are good children, Father Christmas will fill them with presents,' their mother told them.

Now it is early on Christmas morning, and the children have just woken up.

JACKIE: Wake up, Sheila. He's come! Father Christmas has come!

SHEILA: He's brought me such a lot of presents. I've got a doll's house and three books and some coloured pencils and a lot of other things. What have you got?

JACKIE: I've got a new football and a box of soldiers and some books.

SHEILA: What's in your stocking?

JACKIE: Some sweets and an orange and an apple and a ten penny piece and lots of other things.

SHEILA: Shall we get up now?

JACKIE: No, we'll stay in bed and play with our toys.

MRS BROWN: Wake up, everyone. It's Christmas morning. Who's going to church this morning?

MR BROWN: Tony and I will take David, Susan and the children, if you and Brenda cook the dinner.

MRS BROWN: All right. Then we can have some games for the children this afternoon, after we've seen the Queen on television.

BRENDA: Doesn't the Christmas tree look nice? You've done it very well this year.

SUSAN: There's a present on it for everyone. David and I put them on yesterday. We'll have the presents from the tree after tea.

MR BROWN: Hurry up. If we don't hurry, we'll be late for church. The bells are ringing.

For Christmas dinner they had turkey and Christmas pudding. In the afternoon they watched the Queen on television, then the older people rested while the younger ones played games with the children. In England most people spend Christmas Day at home with their families, especially if they have small children.

BRENDA (*after tea*): Now children, Father Christmas has brought you a lot of presents, and you've had another one from the tree, and now it's time for bed.

SHEILA: What a nice Christmas. I shall take my new doll to bed with me.

JACKIE: I think I've eaten too much.

TONY: You'll be all right in the morning, if you go to sleep at once. And tomorrow we're going to the pantomime.

JACKIE: Oh, good! Can I sit next to David? He always makes me laugh.

BRENDA: Yes, if you want to. Now, come on, up to bed!

MRS BROWN: Oh dear! I'm so tired.

MR BROWN: The children have enjoyed it. And Christmas is the children's day. We'll have a drink and then a game of cards.

SUSAN: Sit down by the fire, Mother. You must be tired. David and I'll make the supper.

TONY: And Brenda and I will do the washing up.

Answer these questions:

1 If today is Christmas Eve, what will tomorrow be?
2 What do English people give to their friends on Christmas Day?
3 What do people see if they come into the Browns' house at Christmas?
4 What do children think Father Christmas will do if they are good?
5 What do children do if they wake up early on Christmas morning?
6 What will you have for Christmas dinner if you are in England?
7 Where do most English people spend Christmas if they have small children?
8 Who does Jackie want to sit next to when they go to the pantomine?
9 Why was Mrs Brown tired?

New Words

bedtime ('bedtaim)
a branch (braːntʃ)
a card (kaːd)
children ('tʃildrən)
a chimney ('tʃimni)
a cousin ('kʌzn)
a doll (dɔl)
a drink (driŋk)
eve (iːv)
holly ('hɔli)
a pantomime ('pæntəmaim)
a present ('prezənt)
a pudding ('pudiŋ)
a soldier ('souldʒə)
a stocking ('stɔkiŋ)
a toy (tɔi)
a turkey ('təːki)
the washing-up ('wɔʃiŋ'ʌp)

Brenda ('brendə)
Christmas ('krisməs)
Jackie ('dʒæki)
Mason ('meisn)
Sheila ('ʃiːlə)
Tony ('touni)

to hang, hung (hæŋ, hʌŋ)
to laugh, laughed (laːf, laːft)
to rest, rested (rest, 'restid)

especially (i'speʃəli)
exciting (ik'saitiŋ)
gay (gei)
if (if)
over ('ouvə)
such (sʌtʃ)

Sentence Patterns

53 Condition clauses—'If'

Most people spend Christmas at home if they have small children.
A football crowd is happy if their team scores a goal.
Mrs Brown goes shopping on Monday if it isn't raining.
If you listen carefully you can hear the sea from here.

We shall go to the sea tomorrow if it is fine.
You'll be all right in the morning if you rest now.
If you are good children Father Christmas will bring you some presents.
If you don't hurry we'll be late for church.

Exercises

A. Write answers to these questions, beginning *If* ...

1 If Jackie and Sheila wake up early on Christmas morning, what will they do?
2 If it is Christmas Day, what will Mrs Brown cook for dinner?
3 If the children are good, what do they think Father Christmas will bring them?
4 If they switch on the television on Christmas afternoon, who will they see?
5 If the Browns go to the theatre on the day after Christmas, what will they see?
6 If families in England have small children, where do they usually spend Christmas?
7 If you drop a glass on a stone floor, what happens?
8 If you go out in the rain, what happens?

B. In some of these sentences the relative (*who* or *which*) could be left out. Write these sentences.

1 David has a motor-bike which he bought last year.
2 People who eat too much usually get fat.
3 Is this the road which goes to Strawberry Farm?
4 Do you know the man who I was speaking to?
5 These are the people who went on holiday with us last year.
6 I'm waiting for the bus which goes to Bishopton.
7 Thank you for the present which you sent me.
8 He is a man who speaks politely to everyone.

9   This is the book which I have been looking for.
10   I gave her the present which I had from the Christmas tree.

C. Make these sentences negative:

1   Tom and Susan drove home in Mr Brown's car.
2   Tom always drives carefully.
3   Tom drove carefully this afternoon.
4   Susan told him to look at the road.
5   In this picture he's looking at the road in front of him.
6   He ran into the other car.
7   Susan was hurt.
8   But she enjoyed her drive home.
9   They told Mrs Brown about it that evening.
10   Careful drivers drive fast through towns.

D. Put the right preposition into each of the blanks in this passage:

This is a picture ... Buckingham Palace. The Palace is ... London ...
Victoria Station. A policeman is standing ... the gate, and a car is driving

... the gate ... the Palace. There is a flag ... the car. It is the Queen's flag, and she is ... the car. Some people are standing ... the gate; they have some children ... them. There is a soldier ... the policeman. A man is taking ... his hat.

a flag (flæg)

E. Finish each of these sentences with a time clause beginning *when, while, before, after* or *until:*

1   We will stay here ...
2   Susan will go home ...
3   The children will go to bed ...
4   No one can have lunch ...
5   David will spend a week on the farm ...
6   We met the Brown family ...
7   We usually have dinner ...
8   I left my car outside the restaurant ...
9   'Please take off your shoes ...'
10 They all ran into their tents ...

F. *Write about Christmas, or some other holiday, in your own country.*

List of Irregular Verbs

(a)   *Past Participle same as Past tense*

bring	brought	brought
build	built	built
buy	bought	bought
can	could	
catch	caught	caught
cost	cost	cost
cut	cut	cut
dig	dug	dug
find	found	found
get	got	got
hang	hung	hung
have	had	had
hear	heard	heard
hit	hit	hit
keep	kept	kept
leave	left	left
lend	lent	lent
let	let	let
make	made	made
meet	met	met
pay	paid	paid
put	put	put
read	read	read
say	said	said
sell	sold	sold
set off	set off	set off
shall	should	
shine	shone	shone
shut	shut	shut
sit	sat	sat
spend	spent	spent
stand	stood	stood
strike	struck	struck
tell	told	told
think	thought	thought
will	would	
win	won	won

(b)   *Past Participle different from Past tense*

begin	began	begun
blow	blew	blown
break	broke	broken
come	came	come
do	did	done
drink	drank	drunk
drive	drove	driven
eat	ate	eaten
fall	fell	fallen
forget	forgot	forgotten
give	gave	given
go	went	gone
grow	grew	grown
is	was	been
know	knew	known
lie	lay	lain
ride	rode	ridden
ring	rang	rung
run	ran	run
see	saw	seen
show	showed	shown
sing	sang	sung
speak	spoke	spoken
swim	swam	swum
take	took	taken
throw	threw	thrown
wake	woke	woken
wear	wore	worn
write	wrote	written

List of Sentence Patterns

Index to the Exercises

Word List

This list gives all the words used in *New Present Day English* Book One, except numbers. The number after each word refers to the unit in which it first appears.

a (ə) 1
about (ə'baut) 9
across (ə'krɔs) 5
after ('ɑːftə) 11
an afternoon
   ('ɑːftə'nuːn) 8
again (ə'gein) 11
age (eidʒ) 10
ago (ə'gou) 16
all (ɔːl) 5
along (ə'lɔŋ) 14
already (ɔːl'redi) 15
always ('ɔːlweiz) 10
an ambulance
   ('æmbjuːləns) 12
among (ə'mʌŋ) 11
an (ən) 3
and (ænd, ənd, ən) 1
angry ('æŋgri) 7
another (ə'nʌðə) 12
to answer ('ɑːnsə) 9
any ('eni) 11
anything ('eniθiŋ) 8
an apple ('æpl) 10
April ('eipril) 15
an arm (ɑːm) 7
to arrange (ə'reindʒ) 13
to arrive (ə'raiv) 17
to ask (ɑːsk) 7
asleep (ə'sliːp) 14
at once (ət 'wʌns) 17
August ('ɔːgəst) 15
an aunt (ɑːnt) 15
   auntie ('ɑːnti)
the autumn ('ɔːtəm) 12

away (ə'wei) 7
baby ('beibi) 16
back (bæk) 9
bacon ('beikən) 3
a bag (bæg) 2
a baker ('beikə) 10
a ball (bɔːl) 18
a bank (bæŋk) 7
a bar (bɑː) 8
a barbecue
   ('bɑːbikjuː) 8
to bark (bɑːk) 15
a basket ('bɑːskit) 15
to be (biː)
   am (æm, əm) 1
   are (ɑː) 1
   been (biːn) 13
   is (iz) 1
   was (wɔz, wəz) 5
   were (wəː, wə) 5
beautiful
   ('bjuːtiful) 16
because (bi'kɔz) 18
a bed (bed) 5
bedclothes
   ('bedklouðz) 17
a bedroom
   ('bedruːm) 15
bedtime
   ('bedtaim) 19
beer (biə) 8
before (bi'fɔː) 11
to begin (bi'gin) 8
   began (bi'gæn)
   begun (bi'gʌn)

behind (bi'haind) 11
a bell (bel) 11
best (best) 18
better ('betə) 18
between (bi'twiːn) 11
a bicycle ('baisikl) 10
big (big) 3
a bill (bil) 13
a bird (bəːd) 1
black (blæk) 6
a blouse (blauz) 11
to blow (blou) 17
  blew (bluː)
  blown (bloun)
blue (bluː) 7
a boat (bout) 16
a book (buk) 1
a booking-clerk
  ('bukiŋklaːk) 6
a booking-office
  ('bukiŋɔfis) 6
a box (bɔks) 6
a boy (bɔi) 3
a boy-friend
  ('bɔifrend) 5
a branch (braːntʃ) 19
bread (bred) 3
to break (breik) 7
  broke (brouk)
  broken ('broukn)
breakfast
  ('brekfəst) 3
a bridge (bridʒ) 16
brightly ('braitli) 15
to bring (briŋ) 6
  brought (brɔːt)
a brother ('brʌðə) 3
brown (braun) 10
to build (bild) 16
  built (bilt)
a building ('bildiŋ) 16
to burn (bəːn) 8

a bus (bʌs) 10
busily ('bizili) 14
busy ('bizi) 9
but (bʌt, bət) 5
butter ('bʌtə) 3
to buy (bai) 6
  bought (bɔːt)
by (bai) 6

a cabbage ('kæbidʒ) 10
a cake (keik) 5
to call (kɔːl) 18
camping
  ('kæmpiŋ) 17
can (kæn) 14
could (kud)
a car (kaː) 4
a card (kaːd) 19
careful ('kɛəfl) 5
a carpet ('kaːpit) 3
to carry ('kæri) 6
to catch (kætʃ) 18
  caught (kɔːt)
a chair (tʃɛə) 1
a chance (tʃaːns) 18
change (tʃeindʒ) 10
cheese (tʃiːz) 9
a cherry ('tʃeri) 15
  cherries
a chicken ('tʃikin) 15
children ('tʃildrən) 19
a chimney ('tʃimni) 19
a chocolate ('tʃɔkələt) 15
Christmas
  ('krisməs) 19
a church (tʃəːtʃ) 14
a cigarette (sigə'ret) 1
a cinema ('sinəmə) 13
a city ('siti) 16
a class (klaːs) 12
a classroom
  ('klaːsruːm) 12

clean (kliːn) 10
clever ('klevə) 18
to close (klouz) 6
clothes (klouðz) 11
a club (klʌb) 18
a coat (kout) 4
coffee ('kɔfi) 3
cold (kould) 4
coloured ('kʌləd) 13
to come (kʌm) 5
  came (keim) 6
  come (kʌm)
a company
  ('kʌmpəni) 11
a conductor
  (kən'dʌktə) 18
a cook (kuk) 8
to cook (kuk) 8
cool (kuːl) 15
corn (kɔːn) 15
a corner ('kɔːnə) 7
to cost (kɔst) 10
  cost (kɔst)
the country
  ('kʌntri) 15
a cousin ('kʌzn) 19
a cow (kau) 15
cricket ('krikit) 12
to cross (krɔs) 15
a crowd (kraud) 18
to cry (krai) 17
  cried (kraid)
a cup (kʌp) 3
a cupboard ('kʌbəd) 12
a customer
  ('kʌstəmə) 10
to cut (kʌt) 14
  cut (kʌt)

a dance (daːns) 9
to dance (daːns) 8
dark (daːk) 11

a daughter ('dɔːtə) 3
a day (dei) 8
dear (diə) 17
December
  (di'sembə) 15
to decide (di'said) 13
a desk (desk) 11
to die (dai) 16
different ('difrənt) 14
difficult ('difiklt) 18
to dig (dig) 14
  dug (dʌg)
a dining-room
  ('daininruːm) 3
dinner ('dinə) 9
dirt (dəːt) 14
a disc jockey
  ('disk 'dʒɔki) 13
a discotheque
  ('diskoutek) 13
a dish (diʃ) 14
to do (duː) 3
  did (did)
  done (dʌn)
a dog (dɔg) 1
a doll (dɔl) 19
a door (dɔː) 1
down (daun) 3
downstairs
  ('daun'stɛəz) 9
a dozen ('dʌzn) 11
a drink (driŋk) 19
to drink (driŋk) 3
  drank (dræŋk)
  drunk (drʌŋk)
to drive (draiv) 5
  drove (drouv) 6
  driven ('drivn)
a driver ('draivə) 7
to drop (drɔp) 16
dry (drai) 10
during ('djuːriŋ) 17

each (iːtʃ) 10
early ('əːli) 7
east (iːst) 17
easy ('iːzi) 16
to eat (iːt) 3
    ate (eit)
    eaten ('iːtn)
an egg (eg) 3
    electric (i'lektrik) 14
    empty ('empti) 9
an end (end) 8
an engine ('endʒin) 17
to enjoy (in'dʒɔi) 8
    enough (i'nʌf) 12
    especially
      (i'speʃəli) 19
eve (iːv) 19
an evening ('iːvniŋ) 8
every ('evri) 10
    everyone
      ('evriwʌn) 16
    everything
      ('evriθiŋ) 8
except (ik'sept) 13
    exciting
      (ik'saitiŋ) 19
an exercise
    ('eksəsaiz) 12
    expensive
      (ik'spensiv) 13

a face (feis) 7
a factory ('fæktri) 10
to fall (fɔːl) 7
    fell (fel)
    fallen ('fɔːln)
a family ('fæmili) 14
    far (faː) 18
a fare (fɛə) 18
a farm (faːm) 15
a farmer ('faːmə) 15

a farmhouse
    ('faːmhaus) 15
a farmyard
    ('faːmjaːd) 15
fast (faːst) 5
fat (fæt) 5
a father ('faːðə) 3
favourite ('feivrit) 17
February
    ('februəri) 15
a field (fiːld) 12
to fill (fil) 12
fine (fain) 14
to find (faind) 9
    found (faund)
a finger ('fiŋgə) 6
to finish ('finiʃ) 12
a fire (faiə) 3
    first (fəːst) 11
a flag (flæg) 19
the, a floor (flɔː) 12
a flower ('flauə) 8
food (fuːd) 15
a foot (fut) 9
    feet (fiːt)
football ('futbɔːl) 12
for (fɔː, fə) 5
to forget (fə'get) 10
    forgot (fə'gɔt)
    forgotten (fə'gɔtn)
a fork (fɔːk) 3
    fresh (freʃ) 10
Friday ('fraidi) 10
a friend (frend) 5
to frighten ('fraitn) 16
from (frɔm, frəm) 4
fruit (fruːt) 10
full (ful) 18

a game (geim) 12
a garage ('gæraːʒ,
    'gæridʒ) 11

a garden ('gɑːdn) 8
gas (gæs) 14
a gate (geit) 4
gay (gei) 19
to get (get) 6
got (gɔt)
a girl (gəːl) 3
a girl-friend
('gəːlfrend) 9
to give (giv) 4
gave (geiv)
given ('givn)
a glass (glɑːs) 9
a glove (glʌv) 4
to go (gou) 4
went (went) 6
gone (gɔn)
a goal (goul) 18
good (gud) 3
better ('betə)
best (best)
good-bye
(gud'bai) 4
good-looking
('gud'lukiŋ) 9
the government
('gʌvənmənt) 13
grass (grɑːs) 8
green (griːn) 13
a greengrocer
('griːngrousə) 10
grey (grei) 16
the ground (graund) 17
to grow (grou) 14
grew (gruː)
grown (groun)
a guitar (gi'tɑː) 14

hair (hɛə) 7
half (hɑːf) 11
half-way
('hɑːf 'wei) 13

half-time
('hɑːf 'taim) 18
a hall (hɔːl) 13
a hand (hænd) 2
a handbag
('hænd'bæg) 13
to hang (hæŋ) 19
hung (hʌŋ)
to happen ('hæpən) 13
happy ('hæpi) 5
happily ('hæpili) 14
hard (hɑːd) 13
to harvest ('hɑːvist) 15
a hat (hæt) 4
to have got (hæv gɔt) 2
has (hæz)
had (hæd) 5
hay (hei) 15
he (hiː, hi) 1
a head (hed) 7
to hear (hiə) 11
heard (həːd)
hello (he'lou) 1
help (help) 13
to help (help) 14
her[1] (həː, hə) 2
her[2] (həː, hə) 9
here (hiə) 3
hers (həːz) 12
him (him) 9
his[1] (hiz) 2
his[2] (hiz) 12
to hit (hit) 7
hit (hit)
a hole (houl) 18
a holiday ('hɔlidi) 11
holly ('hɔli) 19
home (houm) 5
homework
('houmwəːk) 12
to hope (houp) 13
hot (hɔt) 8

a house (haus) 2
how (hau) 10
hungry ('hʌŋgri) 3
to hurry ('hʌri) 5
hurt (həːt) 7
a husband
('hʌzbənd) 4

I (ai) 1
if (if) 19
important
(im'pɔːtənt) 11
in (in) 2
in front of (in
'frʌnt əv) 5
inside (in'said) 6
instead (in'sted) 14
interesting
('intrəstiŋ) 16
into ('intu) 4
iron ('aiən) 8
an iron ('aiən) 14
it (it) 1
its (its) 3

a Jaguar ('dʒægjuə) 5
January
('dʒænuəri) 15
jeans (dʒiːnz) 14
a jewel ('dʒuəl) 16
juice (dʒuːs) 13
July (dʒu'lai) 15
June (dʒuːn) 15
just (dʒʌst) 15

to keep (kiːp) 14
kept (kept)
a kettle ('ketl) 14
a key (kiː) 9
to kick (kik) 17
kind (kaind) 11
a king (kiŋ) 16

a kitchen ('kitʃn) 13
a knife (naif) 3
knives (naivz)
to know (nou) 10
knew (njuː)
known (noun)

lager ('laːgə) 13
large (laːdʒ) 6
last (laːst) 11
late (leit) 6
later ('leitə) 15
to laugh (laːf) 19
lazy ('leizi) 14
to leave (liːv) 6
left (left)
left (left) 16
a leg (leg) 18
to lend (lend) 15
lent (lent)
a lesson ('lesn) 12
to let (let) 16
let (let)
a letter ('letə) 3
to lie (lai) 17
lay (lei)
lain (lein)
life (laif) 17
a light (lait) 9
like (laik) 14
to like (laik) 11
to listen ('lisn) 12
little ('litl) 3
to live (liv) 10
a loaf (louf) 10
loaves (louvz)
to lock (lɔk) 13
long (lɔŋ) 14
to look (luk) 8
the Lord Mayor
('lɔːd 'mɛə) 16
a lot (lɔt) 7

loud (laud) 13
loudly ('laudli) 18
lovely ('lʌvli) 15
luggage ('lʌgidʒ) 6
a lunch (lʌntʃ) 11

madam ('mædəm) 6
to make (meik) 8
made (meid)
a man (mæn) 1
men (men) 6
to manage
    ('mænidʒ) 15
a manager
    ('mænidʒə) 7
many ('meni) 8
a map (mæp) 12
March (maːtʃ) 15
a market ('maːkit) 15
marmalade
    ('maːməleid) 3
a match¹ (mætʃ) 6
a match² (mætʃ) 18
a matter ('mætə) 9
May (mei) 15
me (miː, mi) 9
a meal (miːl) 13
meat (miːt) 14
to meet (miːt) 9
met (met)
to mend
    (mend) 13
a mess (mes) 17
the middle ('midl) 16
midnight
    ('midnait) 16
a mile (mail) 10
milk (milk) 17
mine (main) 12
a minute ('minit) 7
miserable
    ('mizrəbl) 17

Miss (mis) 11
a moment
    ('moumənt) 11
Monday ('mʌndi) 10
money ('mʌni) 10
a month (mʌnθ) 11
more (mɔː) 17
a morning ('mɔːniŋ) 5
a mother ('mʌðə) 3
a motor-cycle (motor-
    bike) ('moutəsaikl,
    moutəbaik) 10
the Motor Show
    ('moutə 'ʃou) 13
a mouth (mauθ) 2
to move (muːv) 18
Mr ('mistə) 2
Mrs ('misiz) 2
much (mʌtʃ) 10
music ('mjuːzik) 13
my (mai) 2
a name (neim) 2
near (niə) 3
nearly ('niəli) 15
to need (niːd) 17
new (njuː) 4
a newspaper
    ('njuːzpeipə) 5
next (nekst) 9
nice (nais) 8
a night (nait) 9
no (nou) 1
noise (nɔiz) 14
noisily ('nɔizili) 14
north (nɔːθ) 17
not (nɔt) 1
a note-book
    ('noutbuk) 12
November
    (nou'vembə) 15
now (nau) 3
a number ('nʌmbə) 7

o'clock (ə'klɔk) 9
October (ɔk'toubə) 15
of (ɔv, əv) 6
off (ɔf) 7
an office ('ɔfis) 7
often ('ɔfn, 'ɔftn) 10
old (ould) 4
on (ɔn) 2
an onion ('ʌnjən) 10
only ('ounli) 7
to open ('oupən) 6
open ('oupən) 14
an opening ('oupniŋ) 17
or (ɔː) 4
an orange ('ɔrindʒ) 10
orange ('ɔrindʒ) 13
other ('ʌðə) 11
our (auə) 2
ours (auəz) 12
outside (aut'said) 6
an oven ('ʌvn) 14
over ('ouvə) 19

to pack (pæk) 17
a packet ('pækit) 6
a pan (pæn) 8
a pantomime
   ('pæntəmaim) 19
paper ('peipə) 11
a park (paːk) 16
Parliament
   ('paːləmənt) 7
to pass (paːs) 3
past (paːst) 11
to pay (pei) 13
   paid (peid)
a pear (pɛə) 10
a pen (pen) 1
a pencil ('pensil) 1
a penny ('peni) 10
   pence (pens)
people ('piːpl) 6

perhaps (pə'hæps) 9
petrol ('petrəl) 13
to pick up ('pik 'ʌp) 17
a picture ('piktʃə) 1
a piece (piːs) 15
a pig (pig) 15
a pillar-box
   ('piləbɔks) 5
a pillow ('pilou) 17
a place (pleis) 16
a plate (pleit) 3
a platform ('plætfɔːm) 6
a play (plei) 13
to play (plei) 12
a player ('pleiə) 18
please (pliːz) 3
to point (pɔint) 12
the police (pə'liːs) 9
a policeman
   (pə'liːsmən) 5
polite (pə'lait) 10
a pop-group
   ('pɔpgruːp) 14
a porter ('pɔːtə) 6
a postman
   ('poustmən) 4
a potato (pə'teitou) 10
a pound (paund) 10
a present ('prezənt) 19
pretty ('priti) 3
a pudding ('pudiŋ) 19
to pull (pul) 17
to put (put) 4
   put (put)

a quarter ('kwɔːtə) 11
a queen (kwiːn) 16
a question ('kwestʃn) 7
quick (kwik) 14
quickly ('kwikli) 14
quiet ('kwaiət) 9
quietly ('kwaiətli) 14

a railway ('reilwei) 6
rain (rein) 8
to rain (rein) 8
to read (riːd) 3
    read (red)
ready ('redi) 8
really ('riəli) 16
a record ('rekɔːd) 8
a record-player
    ('rekɔːd 'pleiə) 8
red (red) 11
a referee (refə'riː) 18
to remember
    (ri'membə) 12
to rest (rest) 19
a restaurant
    ('restərɔŋ) 13
return (ri'təːn) 6
to ride (raid) 14
    rode (roud)
    ridden ('ridn)
right[1] (rait) 5
right[2] (rait) 16
to ring (riŋ) 11
    rang (ræŋ)
    rung (rʌŋ)
a river ('rivə) 16
a road (roud) 15
a roof (ruːf) 18
a room (ruːm) 2
a rope (roup) 17
    round (raund) 7
a Rover ('rouvə) 4
royal ('rɔiəl) 16
Rugby Football
    ('rʌgbi 'futbɔːl) 18
rugger ('rʌgə)
to run (rʌn) 6
    ran (ræn)
    run (rʌn)

same (seim) 16

a sandwich
    ('sænwidʒ) 15
Saturday
    ('sætədi) 10
a saucepan
    ('sɔːspən) 14
a saucer ('sɔːsə) 3
a sausage ('sɔsidʒ) 8
to say (sei) 4
    said (sed)
a school (skuːl) 10
to score (skɔː) 18
the sea (siː) 9
a secretary
    ('sekritri) 11
to see (siː) 6
    saw (sɔː)
    seen (siːn)
to sell (sel) 5
    sold (sould) 6
September
    (sep'tembə) 15
a service ('səːvis) 14
to set off ('set 'ɔf) 17
    set off ('set 'ɔf)
shall (ʃæl) 11
she (ʃiː, ʃi) 1
to shine (ʃain) 15
    shone (ʃɔn)
a shirt (ʃəːt) 11
a shoe (ʃuː) 11
a shop (ʃɔp) 5
    shopping ('ʃɔpiŋ) 10
short (ʃɔːt) 5
a shoulder ('ʃouldə) 15
to shout (ʃaut) 7
to show (ʃou) 16
    showed (ʃoud)
    shown (ʃoun)
to shut (ʃʌt) 17
    shut (ʃʌt)
a side (said) 15

to sing (siŋ) 15

    sang (sæŋ)

    sung (sʌŋ)

    single ('siŋgl) 6

    sir (səː) 6

a sister ('sistə) 3

to sit (sit) 3

    sat (sæt)

a sitting-room

    ('sitiŋruːm) 2

a skirt (skəːt) 11

the sky (skai) 8

to slope (sloup) 17

    slow (slou) 5

    slowly ('slouli) 15

    small (smɔːl) 6

to smoke (smouk) 12

so[1] (sou) 5

so[2] (sou) 18

soccer ('sɔkə) 18

    Association Football

    (ə'sousieiʃn

    'futbɔːl)

a soldier ('souldʒə) 19

some (sʌm) 6

someone

    ('sʌmwʌn) 15

something

    ('sʌmθiŋ) 13

sometimes

    ('sʌmtaimz) 10

a son (sʌn) 3

    soon (suːn) 18

    sorry ('sɔri) 5

    south (sauθ) 17

a spade (speid) 14

to speak (spiːk) 3

    spoke (spouk)

    spoken ('spoukn)

to spend (spend) 15

    spent (spent)

a spoon (spuːn) 3

the spring (spriŋ) 12

a stair (stɛə) 16

a stand (stænd) 13

to stand (stænd) 3

    stood (stud)

to start (stɑːt) 8

a station ('steiʃn) 6

to stay (stei) 14

a steak (steik) 8

    still (stil) 14

a stocking ('stɔkiŋ) 19

a stone (stoun) 15

a stop (stɔp) 18

to stop (stɔp) 5

a store (stɔː) 13

a strawberry

    ('strɔːbri) 15

a stream (striːm) 17

a street (striːt) 5

to strike (straik) 16

    struck (strʌk)

    strong (strɔŋ) 18

    such (sʌtʃ) 19

    suddenly ('sʌdnli) 15

    sugar ('ʃugə) 11

a suit (sjuːt) 11

the summer ('sʌmə) 8

the sun (sʌn) 15

to sun-bathe

    ('sʌnbeið) 17

    Sunday ('sʌndi) 10

a surprise (sə'praiz) 15

    sweet (swiːt) 10

a sweet (swiːt) 13

to swim (swim) 14

    swam (swæm)

    swum (swʌm)

to switch (switʃ) 17

a table ('teibl) 1

to take (teik) 4

    took (tuk) 6

taken ('teikn)
to talk (tɔːk) 5
tall (tɔːl) 3
a taxi ('tæksi) 7
tea (tiː) 7
a teacher ('tiːtʃə) 12
a team (tiːm) 18
a telephone
　　('telifoun) 7
to telephone
　　('telifoun) 9
television
　　('telivi3n) 13
to tell (tel) 9
told (tould)
a tent (tent) 17
than (ðæn) 17
thank you
　　('θæŋkjuː) 4
that (ðæt) 1
the (ðə, ði) 2
a theatre ('θiː ətə) 11
their (ðɛə) 2
theirs (ðɛəz) 12
them (ðem) 4
then (ðen) 7
there (ðɛə) 3
these (ðiːz) 1
they (ðei) 1
a thief (θiːf) 9
thieves (θiːvz)
thin (θin) 5
a thing (θiŋ) 9
to think (θiŋk) 15
thought (θɔːt)
thirsty ('θəːsti) 11
this (ðis) 1
those (ðouz) 1
through (θruː) 6
to throw (θrou) 15
threw (θruː)
thrown (θroun)

Thursday
　　('θəːzdi) 10
a ticket ('tikit) 6
tidy ('taidi) 14
to tidy ('taidi) 17
a tie (tai) 11
tired ('taiəd) 13
to (tu, tə) 3
today (tə'dei) 5
together (tə'geðə) 13
a toilet ('tɔilit) 16
tomorrow
　　(tə'mɔrou) 9
tonight (tə'nait) 17
too (tuː) 3
a torch (tɔːtʃ) 17
to touch (tʌtʃ) 17
a tower ('tauə) 16
a town (taun) 5
a Town Hall
　　('taun 'hɔːl) 9
a toy (tɔi) 19
a train (trein) 6
a tree (triː) 8
trousers
　　('trauzəz) 12
a trouser suit
　　('trauzə 'sjuːt) 13
to try (trai) 12
Tuesday ('tjuːzdi) 10
a turkey ('təːki) 19
to type (taip) 11
a typewriter
　　('taipraitə) 11
a tyre ('taiə) 13

an umbrella
　　(ʌm'brelə) 6
an uncle ('ʌŋkl) 15
under ('ʌndə) 2
untidy (ʌn'taidi) 14
until (ʌn'til) 11

up (ʌp) 3
upstairs ('ʌp'stɛəz) 11
us (ʌs) 9
usually ('juːʒuəli) 12

a van (væn) 10
a vegetable
     ('vedʒtəbl) 10
very ('veri) 5
a visit ('vizit) 16
to visit ('vizit) 11

to wait (weit) 11
a waiter ('weitə) 13
to wake (weik) 14
     woke (wouk)
     woken ('woukn)
to walk (wɔːk) 3
a wall (wɔːl) 1
to want (wɔnt) 10
     warm (wɔːm) 4
to wash (wɔʃ) 13
a washing-machine
     ('wɔʃiŋmə'ʃiːn) 14
the washing-up
     ('wɔʃiŋ 'ʌp) 19
to waste (weist) 12
a watch (wɔtʃ) 11
to watch (wɔtʃ) 13
     water ('wɔːtə) 17
to wave (weiv) 4
we (wiː, wi) 2
to wear (wɛə) 11
     wore (wɔː)
     worn (wɔːn)
Wednesday
     ('wenzdi) 10
a week (wiːk) 10
a week-end
     ('wiːkend) 14
well (wel) 5
west (west) 16

wet (wet) 8
what (wɔt) 1
a wheel (wiːl) 6
when[1] (wen) 10
when[2] (wen) 16
where (wɛə) 2
which (witʃ) 15
while (wail) 16
a whistle ('wisl) 18
white (wait) 6
who[1] (huː) 4
who[2] (huː) 15
why (wai) 9
a wife (waif) 4
     wives (waivz)
will (wil) 11
to win (win) 18
     won (wʌn)
the wind (wind) 17
a window ('windou) 1
wine (wain) 8
the winter ('wintə) 12
with (wið) 5
without (wið'aut) 11
a woman ('wumən) 1
     women ('wimin) 6
a wood (wud) 17
work (wəːk) 9
to work (wəːk) 7
worried ('wʌrid) 13
to write (rait) 7
     wrote (rout)
     written ('ritn)
     wrong (rɔŋ) 10

a year (jiə) 10
yes (jes) 1
yesterday ('jestədi) 5
you (juː, ju) 1
young (jʌŋ) 8
your (jɔː, jə) 2
yours (jɔːz) 12

Names of Places

Bishopton ('biʃəptən)
Buckingham Palace
  ('bʌkiŋəm 'pælis)
Cardiff ('kɑːdif)
Charing Cross ('tʃærin
  'krɔs)
Chelsea ('tʃelsi)
Earls Court ('əːlz 'kɔːt)
Easthampton
  ('iːsthæmptən)
Edinburgh ('edinbrə)
England ('iŋglənd)
English ('iŋgliʃ)
Fleet Street ('fliːt 'striːt)
Glasgow ('glɑːzgou)
Great Britain ('greit
  'britn)
Holland ('hɔlənd)
Houses of Parliament
  ('hauzis əv 'pɑːləmənt)
Ireland ('aiələnd)
Irishman ('aiəriʃmən)
Leeds (liːdz)
Liverpool ('livəpuːl)
London ('lʌndən)
Manchester ('mæntʃestə)
Mansion House (the)
  ('mænʃən 'haus)

National Gallery (the)
  ('næʃnəl 'gæləri)
Oxford Street ('ɔksfəd
  'striːt)
Paris ('pæris)
Piccadilly Circus
  ('pikədili 'səːkəs)
Roman ('roumən)
St Paul's Cathedral (sənt
  'pɔːlz kə'θiːdrəl)
Scotland ('skɔtlənd)
Soho ('souhou)
Southampton
  (sauθ'æmptən)
Strand (the) (strænd)
Switzerland
  ('switsələnd)
Thames (the)
  (temz)
Tower (the) ('tauə)
Trafalgar Square
  (trə'fælgə 'skwɛə)
Victoria Station
  (vik'tɔːriə 'steiʃn)
Wales (weilz)
Westminster Abbey
  ('westminstə 'æbi)
Whitehall ('waithɔːl)

Boys' Names

Anthony (Tony)
('æntəni, 'touni)
Benjamin (Ben)
('bendʒəmin, ben)
David ('deivid)
Frederick (Fred)
('fredrik, fred)
George (dʒɔːdʒ)
James (Jim) (dʒeimz,
dʒim)

Jack (Jackie) (dʒæk,
'dʒæki)
John (dʒɔn)
Joseph (Joe) ('dʒouzif,
dʒou)
Paddy ('pædi)
Peter ('piːtə)
Thomas (Tom) ('tɔməs,
tɔm)
Toby ('toubi)

Girls' Names

Brenda ('brendə)
Ethel ('eθəl)
Helen ('helin)
Joan (dʒoun)

Mary ('mɛəri)
Sheila ('ʃiːlə)
Susan ('suːzn)

Family Names

Barnes (baːnz)
Blake (bleik)
Brook (bruk)
Brown (braun)
Campbell ('kæmbəl)
Jones (dʒounz)
Mason ('meisn)

Morton ('mɔːtn)
Robinson ('rɔbinsən)
Smith (smiθ)
Stansbury ('stænzbri)
Stephens ('stiːvənz)
Thompson ('tɔmsn)

'Teaching Words' in this Book

adjective ('ædʒiktiv)
adverb ('ædvəːb)
answer ('aːnsə)
blank (blæŋk)
bracket ('brækit)
choose (tʃuːz)
clause (kloːz)
comparison
   (kəm'pærisən)
condition (kən'diʃn)
continuous (kən'tinjuəs)
conversation
   (kɔnvə'seiʃn)
correct (kə'rekt)
date (deit)
different ('difrənt)
example (ik'zaːmpl)
expect (ik'spekt)
form (foːm)
future ('fjuːtʃə)
hour (auə)
imperative (im'perətiv)
impersonal (im'pəːsənəl)
infinitive (in'finitiv)
irregular (i'regjulə)
join (dʒɔin)
list (list)
mark (maːk)

minute ('minit)
negative ('negətiv)
objective (əb'dʒektiv)
page (peidʒ)
participle ('paːtisipl)
passage ('pæsidʒ)
pattern ('pætən)
perfect ('pəːfikt)
personal ('pəːsnəl)
plural ('pluːrəl)
possessive (pə'zesiv)
preposition (prepə'ziʃn)
present ('prezənt)
pronoun ('prounaun)
reason ('riːzn)
regular ('regjulə)
relative ('relətiv)
sentence ('sentəns)
simple ('simpl)
tag (tæg)
tense (tens)
time (taim)
time-table ('taimteibl)
use (juːz)
verb (vəːb)
weather ('weðə)
word (wəːd)